MYSTIC TRENDS IN JUDAISM

MYSTIC TRENDS IN JUDAISM

BY
ARNOLD POSY

jD | Jonathan David Publishers, Inc.
Middle Village, New York 11379

MYSTIC TRENDS IN JUDAISM

by

Arnold Posy

Jonathan David Publishers, Inc.
68-22 Eliot Avenue
Middle Village, NY 11379

1995 1997 1998 1996 1994
2 4 6 8 10 9 7 5 3 1

Library of Congress Cataloging-in-Publication Data

Posy, Arnold,
      Mystic trends in Judaism. New York, J. David
      213 p. 23cm.

           1. Mysticism—Judaism 2. Jewish sects. I. Title
      BM723.P65   296.8'33   66-21592
                                                               MARC
ISBN 978-0-8246-0473-8

Book design by Jennifer Vignone
Printed in the United States of America

To my daughter and son-in-law
Deena Myra and H. Reed Metzger
with all my love

Acknowledgement

With deep gratitude I thank Joseph Leftwich for his invaluable help in revising and translating these essays, with the exception of *Rome, Jerusalem and Nazareth* and some Notes and Additions.

–A. Posy

CONTENTS

BELIEF IN JUDAISM IN A GENERATION OF DISBELIEF

*W*HAT IS essential in Judaism? It is one of the fundamental questions often posed by thinking people. There are a number of different answers, and not all the answers agree. But I won't go into that now. I want to deal with only two of the answers, that nobody questions and all people accept. One answer was given by Hillel—Hillel the Prince, Hillel the Elder—who lived some two thousand years ago, one of the greatest teachers and sages in the history of Judaism. His answer was given to a heathen who later turned proselyte. "What is hateful to you, do not to your fellow-man. This is the whole Law. The rest is commentary."

It means that Hillel based Judaism on the humanistic, ethical, social and moral relations that the Torah has established between man and man.

But about twelve centuries later there arose another great Jewish thinker, Rambam, Moses ben Maimon, Maimonides; and he formulated not one, but thirteen principles of Judaism, thirteen articles of faith. He went much further than Hillel. He brought in also those relationships which Ju-

11

daism has established between God and man.

Of course, Maimonides did not reject Hillel's Golden Rule. He only added to Hillel's humanistic principle of Judaism. It had been enough to maintain Judaism in Hillel's day. Then the dominant power had been heathen Rome, whose basic principle of civilization was Might is Right. Therefore, Hillel had established the Jewish thesis—Justice is Right. But in Maimonides' time, when both Christians and Moslems preached (even if they did not always practice) humanistic relations between man and man, Hillel's sole principle of Judaism was no longer sufficient to hold Jews to their faith and to withstand the afflictions that were heaped on them because of their religion.

Not so the principles that Maimonides added. These filled successive generations of Jews with so much fervor that our sons and daughters endured endless sufferings, let themselves be martyred for His Name's Sake, and did not depart from them. What was the source of this great, unusual, inexhaustible strength?

It came from their deep belief in the cardinal principle, "Know before Whom you will in future have to give account and reckoning" (Ethics of Our Fathers). It is this that Maimonides stressed as the essential in Judaism. The account and reckoning is to be given to the Holy One Blessed be He! And this thought, that *in time* account and reckoning would have to be given to the Holy One Blessed be He, became later on even firmer and more resolute with the belief that this account and reckoning would have to be given *always*. Jews had this in mind, day and night, wherever they were, wherever they turned—"Know before Whom you stand." This became their one idea in life, which they never ceased to repeat, both in uttered word and in the deepest depths of the hidden places in their minds, *Know* and never stop knowing before Whom you stand, before the Creator, as Maimonides defined Him, "the Creator Blessed be His

Name, Who knows every deed of the children of men and all their thoughts, Who is One, and there is no Oneness, no Unity in any manner like His, and He *was, is* and *will be*."

But—and we must not let ourselves be deceived in this regard—many of the Children of Israel in this generation have been infected by disbelief and denial—some more, some less—in regard to this *Know,* this Know before Whom you stand, and to Whom you will have to give account and reckoning for your deeds.

It is because they no longer consider the *Who* as something personal, subjective, directly concerning themselves, but from an objective philosophical aspect, often only a hypothesis, with a considerable dose of skepticism.

Now let us admit, without going deeper into the matter, that the disbelievers have a right to think as they do, and that logic is on their side, so that they may, therefore, cease to repeat the *"Know* before *Whom* you stand" and "Before *Whom* you will have to give account and reckoning."

But those of them who have eyes to see and senses to feel, come bang up against this *"Know,"* though in a different form—instead of "Know before *Whom* you stand," it is before *What* you stand."

This *What* has bearing on everything, and all that we meet in Nature, all of the wonders of Nature, from the atom to the cosmos, and to the wonder of life as a whole, above all man.

Let us begin with the atom. It was considered the absolute smallest particle in physical nature, which could not be split or divided. Now science has discovered that the atom is a highly complex system of smaller particles, and the more we learn about it, the more wonderful and mysterious it all becomes. The world of the atom is so fantastic that what we have come to know about it has forced science to revise its ideas about Space and Time.

The atom is so small, science tells us, that if a drop of

water were to be magnified to the size of the whole earth, each separate atom in the drop would be no larger than a cherry. One drop of water consists of billions and billions of atoms. And the wonderful thing about it is that the atom itself is composed of many parts. The atomic structure is compared with our whole solar system, around which revolve the planets, of which our earth is one. The same is true of the atom. It, too, has a center, its nucleus, round which revolve the electrons in the same way as the planets around the sun. And it all goes according to a pre-ordained order, a specific law like that which controls the planets revolving round the sun.

And these electrons, small almost to the point of non-existence, create for us the conditions by which we have radio, television, and all the different electrical gadgets that we use in our daily life.

These electrons revolve round the center, the core of the atom. Now what is this core? It is, too, not one substance. It also consists—as far as we know—of a large number of different parts that hold together so firmly that if we divide them it creates a terrific force that we know as the horror of the atom bomb.*

---

* What is even more amazing, is the accepted scientific theory that the atom, resembling a solar system in miniature, is nearly all empty space. The diameter of the electrons, the "planets" of the atom's "solar system," is approximately one fifty thousandth (1/50,000) part of the diameter of the whole atom—that is, the diameter of the orbit in which the uttermost electron is revolving. The diameter of the nucleus is about the same as that of an electron. Mathematically, this leads to the conclusion that if all the atoms of a man's body were so condensed as to leave no unfilled space, the man's body would become a barely visible speck.

Interesting to note the comments on this subject by one who seems to have stated it most clearly for our present needs— Prof. Donald Hatch Andrews of the Department of Chemistry, Johns Hopkins University. He joins many of the greatest scientific thinkers who have expressed themselves about the enigmas arising from the splitting of the atom and the dissolution

These small almost nothings in size are the bricks, the building materials, of which the entire cosmos is constituted, with all that is contained in the cosmos. And it is all shrouded in such impenetrable mystery, that the human mind cannot fathom it. Just as the human mind is unable to fathom the cosmos, which consists of billions and billions of galaxies, each composed of countless billions of stars, of which each star is a sun like our sun, with planets and comets, on some of which, it is surmised, life has developed, with living beings, as on earth.

So WE SEE and we feel with all our senses the sheer Wonder of the world, the vast miracle and miracles of Nature. At the same time we become aware of the vast concealed spiritual powers of man. And it all confronts us with riddles that we cannot possibly solve. They arouse a sense of awe and spiritual exaltation in us.

Therefore, when we become absorbed in the contemplation of these things, even if it does not give us that profound faith in the personal *Who* which the deeply religious people have, it must still leave us standing in wonderment before the *What*, and we are forced to repeat with but little altera-

---

of matter and have found it necessary to revamp and reshape their philosophical outlook in the light of their new scientific concepts. The most prominent among them are: Erwin Schroedinger, Max Planck, Niels Bohr, Henry Margenau, Edmund Sinnott, Albert Einstein and others.

If we were to create a press, said Prof. Andrews, which could squeeze out all the empty space in atoms, "one could squeeze down the entire human race, every man, woman and child on earth, to the point where they could all be put in a bottle which you could slip right in your pocket. That shows how little we amount to in a material way."

Prof. Andrews continues, "If the atom is really mostly empty space filled with a little electricity, and only a tiny speck of matter at its center [and matter itself is actually only waves or vibrations], we have to revise our ideas of what is real. It is clear that we can no longer take our senses as our guides. When my finger touches a piece of wood it is not *matter* touching *matter*;

tion, the words: "Know before What you stand."

In other words: Even if we lose simple faith in the *Holy One*, Blessed be He, we cannot clear our minds of wonderment at the *Holiness*, Blessed be It.

Let us consider the problem from an evolutionary approach: The simple faith of our fathers and forefathers has developed into—according to modern opinion—a rational belief. It means: That faith has in its essentials been retained, though somewhat changed in form, with respect to language and idea. The essential thing is to have *faith*, faith in the worth of man, which Hillel, as we previously noted, established as the central principle of Judaism—in the worth

---

it is an *electrical wave* touching another *electrical wave*. When I look at you, I am not seeing matter; I am seeing a harmonic complex of electrical vibrations. And what is more important, I am seeing far less than one percent of all the vibration which you are producing. For your presence is manifested far more in the invisible world than in the visible. And to understand your *total* reality we must examine this world of invisible vibrations and invisible forces."

These invisible forces are numerous: they are the enigma of gravity, magnetism, light, the thousands of electrical waves which are the carriers of radio and television programs from all over the world, which are constantly passing right through us, and oceans of infra red and thermal waves. Prof. Andrews asserts that, "The atoms in our bodies are giving off radiation of this kind all the time. When we meet, you radiate infra red at me; I radiate it back at you. Every muscle movement, every nerve impulse, every thought results in some wave of this sort." And all of these in essence compose the entire material being of man, and not only of man.

This knowledge, furthermore, leads man to the logical conclusion that there is much more to everything in Nature than we perceive. Man is inevitably awakened to the fact that the world about us exhibits for us only its very limited aspects, and we become conscious that we know very little of what is suspected about the universe and man in the universe. We can, therefore, no longer insist that things do not exist merely because they are not physically exposed to us. Certainly, there is a reality even beyond our human physical senses.

of Nature, and let us say this, too—of Super Nature, the Supernatural. And when we grow conscious of this faith, it becomes transformed into an essential, which *can, must* and *will* hold us to Judaism.

EARNEST, thoughtful religious people have already ceased to conceive God as a jealous, wrathful spirit of whom we must go in fear, to whom we must bow and kneel and keep singing praises, lest He will punish us. This is a God whom people have endowed with human weaknesses and passions, and it is in fact, a profanation of the God-idea.

The Jewish Torah has in the absolute sense taken everything physical out of the realm of the Divine. The Torah prohibits even any physical conception of God. The prohibition was proclaimed in the Decalogue: "Thou shalt not make a graven image, nor the form of anything that is in heaven above or in the earth beneath." It is still more explicit in the warning in Deuteronomy: "Take heed therefore for your souls, for you saw no similitude."

This means that to conceive of God in a physical form is a sin. Maimonides says it in his Thirteen Principles: "That the Creator, Blessed be His Name, is not a body, and that He is free from all that is material, and no imagination can conceive any form for Him."

It is true that the Prophets speak of serving God, of prayers, songs of praise, coming close to God, union with God. "God hears and sees." "God is near to all who call upon Him in truth." These are indeed contradictions, and Jewish thought questions them. How is an approach to God, a union with God, possible if God is beyond all human comprehension? What close relationship can be established between endless eternity, infinity, and mortal limited man?

To which we get the answer that the words of the Prophets are symbolic. The Kabbalists explain it through their idea of Sefiroth. God is so vast and occupies all space, so that nothing is void of Him. He is too vast even to create the universe, for the whole universe is insignificant compared to Him. Then how can we imagine, say the Kabbalists, that God watches over each separate individual, measures his good deeds and his bad, and judges him accordingly?

The answer the Kabbalists give is that only the emanations of God, the Sefiroth, do this, and it is to them we pray. Even they are too vast for this, but there are *Shivrei Keilim*, broken vessels, bits and fragments, and it is from them that everything comes. It is these bits and fragments—let us call them by a modern name, spiritual atoms—that compose world and man.

If so, what is the sense and purpose of prayer? The answer is that prayer is not addressed to God nor even to the Sefiroth, but to the *Shivrei Keilim*, the broken vessels, the bits and fragments. Man prays not for God's sake, but for man's sake. It is not the words of prayer that matter, but the fervor. For this leads man to draw up his spiritual account, to make his spiritual reckoning; it cleanses him from his deeds of error, purifies his soul and unites him with the great mystery of the vast. And when man reaches this stage, he becomes purified, he feels that his concern with the things of this world is trivial, and he rises to the realization that he is a spark in the vast, a spark of God. When he reaches this stage, he becomes worthy of and brings nearer the days of the Messiah.

As for Messiah, he is not a particular person, but an ideal, a symbol. What is important is not Messiah, but Messianism. And Messianism is humanity, all humanity. For Messiah cannot come save in a generation that is wholly good, when each individual will be completely and absolutely righteous. Man's own soul must be saved first, before the saviour can come. There is a particle of Messianism concealed in each man. When all mankind will be dominated by the desire to achieve union with God, Messiah will become universal.

This is the sense in which we must understand Judaism.

Why is Torah holy? It contains a lot of ordinary stories, which are worldly and have nothing to do with holiness. We are told it is not these stories in the Torah that are its true purpose. The stories are only a symbol of the vastness of the world, of which man is the highest expression. What matters is not what is written in the Torah, not the plain meaning of the Torah, but the symbol concealed in it.

Hasidism explains it more precisely:

Out of everything in the world flows the majesty of His Holy Name, even from simple ordinary stories and narratives. This is also the source of worldly song and poetry. People create song—it comes from wonder at God's creation, from the desire to encompass the sublime through the lowly.

"When I join in union with the Divine idea," said the Baal Shem, "I let my tongue speak what it will, even just gibberish. For I connect the speech with His Blessed Name, for each word has a root which transcends the stories." It is the same when it comes to the ways of Nature. "Look up to heaven and count the stars," said one of the Baal Shem's disciples. "Man can see God's sublimity most when he looks up to heaven and sees the course of the stars and the wonderful light they give. That is how man can fill himself full with the wonder of God." "How much greater is the wonder when man considers himself, and comes to realize the wonder of the Divine Spirit that was put into him."

LET US consider the matter from the philosophic aspect. What is man? Did he create himself? Of course not! In the first place, each man is a fortuitous, a chance product of fertility, resulting from the intercourse between man and woman, which is itself a gift that Nature bestowed on man, and man did not put into himself. Secondly: It all comes from something *given* by some outside Power. What is this Power?

Developed human religious thought conceives this Power as Holiness and calls it God. Holiness is infinite. Holiness

is the idea that is beyond and above human frailties.
Can we explain it differently? Man does not create. He
himself is created. He does not even choose, nor find his
own father and mother. They are already there. Nor does he
create the holiness. He finds it already there. So it is plain to
the mind—it must be!—that just as his father and mother
through inheritance, through heredity, give him his body, so
holiness through inheritance gives him his spirit. It means
that man is no more than an episode of Holiness, which religious folk call God—a reflection on the minutest scale of
the Spirit of God.

But we must be careful not to minimize *man*. According
to this reasoning, man, having in him the sparks of Holiness, as God's crowning work in Creation, has learned to
create and control wonderful machinery, in a similar way as
the mechanism of man himself is controlled—for human
bodies are also wonderfully complex machines.

But what makes a machine work? The physical qualities
of a machine are implanted in it by *thought*—through human
thought. *Thought* is the possession of man. But what controls
thought? What creates it? What stimulates it?

When man considers himself in relation to the wonder of
Nature, from the atom to the cosmos, the great mystery of
life, and in general all that Nature has, *Being* and *Not-Being*,
and spiritually a *Super-Being*, the essential fact that his
thought is capable of wonderment at this great wonder, the
essential fact that he can comprehend this wonder—this fact
makes man more wonderful still than all the wonders he
wonders at. What apparatus is there in man that makes it
possible for him to comprehend, wonder and to be able to
think at all?

It is established in human knowledge that it is the brain,
the human brain that creates this possibility for man to
think. But what is the mystery of the human brain? How
does it become possible for these physical, material brain

cells to evoke abstract ideas that are in no way in the category of the physical and the material?

For years and years, human knowledge, science, has been searching the human mind, and it has not yet discovered anything. We still know very little about it. We have found that the brain is composed of billions of cells, but how the cells work, how they produce thoughts, emotions, movements, remains a riddle. We see only the results of the brain's functions, but we have no idea, no knowledge of how it works. We know that the special qualities of their particular brains produced the works of Shakespeare, the visions of Moses and the Prophets, the philosophies of Aristotle, Spinoza, Kant, the marvels of mathematics and physics and logic. But nobody knows how it all happens.

Now the science of parapsychology is stumbling on certain hidden powers of the mind, on powers and qualities that are even more wonderful and marvelous, like the wonders of telepathy. Can a man penetrate into the thoughts of another man? We have accumulated thousands of cases which prove that it does sometimes happen. But *how* does it happen? That remains a mystery.

And the wonder of clairvoyance—the power to see things that are far away from him who sees, even the power to foresee the future. We have not yet come to any final conclusions about these mysterious capacities of the brain. We have no idea of its laws and the way they work. But that there is something to it, we no longer doubt, just as we do not doubt that certain people have certain propensities, certain gifts and talents to write poetry or music or to paint. They need inspiration to do their work. Where do they get their inspiration? Where does it come from?

Nobody knows. A poet can't write songs any time he wants to. He can't just sit down and write poetry. It comes by itself, in its own time. Not when you want it. What is inspiration? Why does inspiration sometimes come and sometimes not? No one has yet found the answer.

We know that there are minds capable of one thing and minds capable of something else. Why? We don't know. Psychologists and psychiatrists search and probe, but these things remain mysteries. How much can a brain absorb? How does it retain things in memory?

Because we don't know, because science is baffled, we must fall back on faith, belief in God, even in Divine Providence that orders the world, in a Mind above mind, a Will above will, a Faculty beyond all our faculties, of which our wildest imagination cannot grasp the smallest, minutest part.

Nature that is all around us is not blind. Its laws and its set and established order are not determined by chance. Somewhere there *must* be an answer to all these questions, to all this wonder that we hit against. If man has been given the faculty of asking questions there must be an answer somewhere to these questions. What is the answer? We don't know. But what we do know, and know with certainty, is that we must have faith, and believe that the answer is there, somewhere. And what holds the answer is Holiness.

Logical thought rejects the assumption that world and life are no more than a self-evolved physical mechanism which came about with no outside influence. There must be this *Thought above thought*, and it is this He, who controls human thought. This *Thought above thought* is and should be the ground-motive to make us recognize if not the *Holy One, Blessed be He*, then at least *Holiness, Blessed be It*.

It does not matter how one conceives Holiness, nor what one calls the Holiness. It may be described in the fashion of the great Kabbalist Rabbi Moses Cordovero, who directly influenced Spinoza in developing his line of metaphysical thought, or for instance, by Ludwig Feuerbach, on whose philosophy Karl Marx constructed his theory of dialectical materialism. The Holiness is in them, too. Even Feuerbach and Marx must stand amazed and baffled before the great mysteries of the world.

Each conception makes sense only if it recognizes the Unity of the Creation. Because all Creation is One—from the atom to the cosmos. All Creation is One.

But one more condition must be added—recognition of the *Holiness of man*. Profanation of man is likened to profanation of God, for man is created in the image of God. There is a spark of God in him.

The substance of man is good. True, a man can be bad, but that is only because something in his make-up has gone wrong, has been spoiled, like a machine, which when any part of it goes wrong, ceases to work properly. The same is true of man. But the essential substance of man is good, is a spark of God.

This idea is the absolute essential of Judaism. Thus the sages have decided that those who have not accepted the severe 613 mitzvoth of Judaism, but only the elementary seven mitzvoth, are counted among the pious, the righteous of the nations, and have a share in the life to come. These are the laws not to worship idols, not to blaspheme God, to establish courts of justice, not to kill, not to commit adultery, not to rob and not to eat flesh cut from a living animal. These are the elementary laws without which no human society can exist. This is in contrast to Christianity, which proclaims that man is by his nature, corrupt and bad, and needs to be saved. It is even more pronounced in the belief of the Hasidim who, according to the teaching of the Baal Shem, hold that a man is still a man even when he has sinned. For sin, they say, is a disease that must be healed, in the same way that madness is a disease that has to be healed.

As for the figure of God, no one can define it. No imagination can picture it. "He has not any form whatsoever," said Maimonides. Not only has God no definable form, but the form of God's Creation, too, is impossible to define.

Each of us had a certain conception of the nature of the universe, and that it was divided into time and space. Then Einstein came and showed us that we were wrong—time and space are not separate spheres, but are relative one to the other. Einstein, who is accounted the greatest scientist in this field, saw more deeply and more widely into the mysteries of nature than any other man before him, or since. And as a result, he was mastered by a feeling of religiousness. "To know," he said, "that what we cannot understand really exists, that it finds expression in the supreme wisdom and the radiant beauty that we with our dull senses can comprehend only in a very primitive way—such knowledge, such feeling, is in the very center of religiousness. It is in this sense, and *only* in this sense, that I belong to the ranks of the truly religious people."

NOW TO what does all this lead? To this, I believe:

Man in general must believe. Without belief, man cannot live in the world. But we are not concerned now with life in general, but with specific Jewish life. In this regard it must be clear to everyone that without belief, one cannot possibly be consciously a Jew.

It is true that there is a tendency among many Jews to retain and maintain their Jewishness vicariously at the expense of, and by virtue of, the belief held by other Jews. They will, for instance, spend Passover at the Seder table of a religious Jew and go into ecstasies over it, though they personally have no belief in the whole story of the Exodus from Egypt and are very skeptical about all that is written in the Haggadah. They have lost their faith in the sounding of the Shofar, in the sanctity of the Sabbath, yet they glorify these things that are observed by the religious Jews, who believe in them heart and soul. The simple faith in the substance of Judaism has gone from them. What they have left is the symbol of Judaism and the reflection of the spiritual ferment in those Jews who have not lost their faith. In other words, they are themselves disbelievers, but they see beauty in those who believe, and they cling to Judaism, to what is beautiful in Judaism, as reflected through those who give life to this beauty.

But this is utterly wrong. True, honest Judaism cannot possibly exist without the foundation of faith. Even if one lacks faith in the God with whom Abraham entered his covenant for all future generations, he can still remain a Jew if he believes in the spiritual values—independent of religion—which are transmitted to us generation after generation, and which go on evolving generation after generation.

That raises a question—how can one believe in Jewish values if one has generally no feeling for high and lofty things of the spirit? How can one be prepared to suffer for Judaism if the mind is incapable of grasping anything that is not plain and clear to common sense thinking, to the ordinary five senses?

The answer is plain—one can't. To be a Jew, one must know what Judaism is. If one can't see the light of the Torah, the hidden light of Judaism, one is not capable of being a Jew.

And here there is a very important point that must be cleared up—when we speak of the light of the Torah, the hidden light of Judaism, we don't mean it particularly in the theological sense. It may be understood, also in the philosophical interpretation of the purpose of everything in the world, or—as Rabbi Nachman Bratzlaver put it—"the world has a Heart."

This follows the logical sequence that one is capable of being a Jew only if one believes in the value of Judaism to such a degree that one can't exchange it for anything else.

Every individual Jew believes—he must believe—in continued Jewish historical and national existence, but not because there is a biological law that distinguishes the Jew from the non-Jew. There is no such law. He believes, too, that Jewish existence has a special spiritual value that makes him hold on to it tenaciously, stubbornly, to such a degree that he cannot give it up, cannot relinquish it under any conditions.

Existence for existence sake is not possible for Jews. An individual can live—even a hard and bitter life—only because he doesn't want to part with life, because he fears death. Not so a people. A people without special spiritual values cannot live. Especially a people like the Jews. We are conscious at every step that our existence as a people makes life for each individual one of us not easier, but harder. We are a people that exposes the life and the welfare of each of its members to peril. Our existence as a people must, therefore, be worth suffering and making sacrifices for.

When can it be worth it? Only when we understand and we feel with a deep inner thrill—such as a pious Jew feels in relation to God—not only that our ancient historic experience is distinguished by something that cannot be found in any other people, but that our present-day life also is a creative continuation that none but we can realize.

Only our deep faith and our consciousness that the moral and spiritual forces which we have accumulated till now and are still accumulating, both for ourselves and for the world, could not have been accumulated by any other peoples, by peoples more secure and living under more stable conditions—only this faith and trust in our creatively spiritual otherness could make it possible for us, the Jewish folk masses, to carry the heavy yoke of self-sacrifice which over the past two thousand years has been the martyr-glory of our history.

When we ponder this matter deeply we must come to the logical conclusion that as a people we Jews must be spiritually creative and in consequence culturally different from other peoples—or we shall cease to be.

And when we say that, we mean not only the Jews in the Diaspora, but also the Jews in the State of Israel. They, too, in the State of Israel, will have no particular value *as a people* if they will be no more than a nation like other nations, if they do not continue the special distinctive character of Jewish culture and Jewish historic experience—from the Prophets to our present creative generation. In this regard it is worth drawing on Jewish historical experience to show that a people such as we, even in our own land, can assimilate—morally.

Let us consider the Prophets. What did they storm and thunder against when their wrath was roused against the nation, if not against the Jewish spiritual and moral assimilation of their generation, which built altars to strange gods? What did the Hasmoneans fight, if not assimilation to the Greeks? As in olden days, so now too, there exists in the Jewish State, the danger of spiritual slavery, slavery in freedom as Achad Ha'am called it. Wherever Jews live we must strain all our spiritual uniqueness. Material boundaries alone, whether in the Diaspora or in the geographical limits of Israel, are not enough for such a people as ours.

The great virtue of having our own land is not, as many of us think, that we can at last fling off the heavy yoke of history and become a nation like all nations. On the contrary, the great virtue is that in our own land we want at last to have a larger and fuller possibility of realizing and developing our cultural-historical uniqueness. It is sad that we so often now hear from Israel foreign-sounding talk, mostly from the youth, that all we have achieved in the two thousand years of Jewish history in developing our national distinctiveness is a kind of punishment from God that must be wiped out, obliterated and forgotten. They want a revolution in the philosophy of life of our people in Israel, to tear out by the roots what they call our "unhealthy ghetto philosophy." They want to cut out of Jewish life the "ghetto mentality," to discard all that has grown to be part of us, over the course of our two thousand years of Galuth life.

To realize how this kind of operation would make Jewish life poorer, we must remember that it would mean dropping the Talmud, the Midrashim, Kabbala, Rambam, Yehuda Halevi, Hasidism and much more that is the very substance and essence of Jewishness.

The whole sense of Judaism, its whole significance, the spirit which feeds and keeps alive the Jewish national soul, developed and became crystallized *more* in the last two thousand years of Galuth than in the first thousand years of our history, living in our own land. The seeds were sown, it is true, in our own land, but they grew and gave fruit in Galuth. Even Moses came from Galuth, from our hard and bitter exile, our bondage in Egypt. Even the Ten Commandments were given to us in the wilderness, on the way to Israel, not in Israel. This holds true for the whole Torah. Moses never entered the Land of Israel. He saw it from afar, never crossed into its borders.

The Prophets lived and preached in Israel, but the fulfillment of their prophecies began only in the Diaspora, in the period of the Tannaim and the Amoraim, among whom there were as many Galuth Jews as Israeli Jews. The Talmud and all those great Jewish spiritual treasures that originated after the completion of the Talmud were the rich heritage of the Gaonim, the Posekim, the Kabbalists, the Payetanim, the Masorites, the philosophers and all the rest who lived and worked in the Galuth and were our great luminaries on our hard road in Galuth. In the period of the Prophets we laid the foundations of Jewish spirituality. But the structure was erected in the Galuth. The Prophet was our dream, the vision, the ideal. The practical realization was in the Galuth. Isaiah's vision was for the end of days. The day to day reality was and remained Mishna, Gemara, Shulchan Aruch,

Zohar, Hasidism—all these holy, radiant shapes that illuminated our difficult Jewish life during the last two thousand years. We became a people of learning, of knowledge, a people with a boundless love of wisdom and study, with a great respect for scholarship, a people of peace and peacefulness.

What is essential in Judaism always remains essential, but we are a people who can adjust ourselves. Without destroying the substance, we adapt modern developments of thought to its fundamental character and its high and lofty character. It sometimes starts a conflict in our own ranks, dividing us into two warring sections. But as time goes on the conflict dies down, and the two sections become reconciled and unity is restored.

Or—if we accept the Hegelian interpretation—the contradiction between thesis and antithesis is resolved by the emergence of the synthesis. We could illustrate this with several examples, but one will be enough—Hasidism and Haskalah. Hasidism stirred all Jewish religious feeling, which was becoming stagnant. It brought in new waves of belief, fed the folk imagination and stimulated individual creative inspiration. Then came Haskalah, as the antithesis of Hasidism, and liberated the people's thought and pointed a road in the direction of modern culture.

The revived religious spirit of one section of Jews and the liberated thought of other sections—this thesis and antithesis—could not dwell together in peace. There was warfare between the two—between Maskilim and Hasidim. It looked like a war to the death; that one side must conquer and the other be destroyed. This is how it appeared in the first half of the nineteenth century. But by the second half of the century, the picture had changed. Two new currents had emerged in Jewish life.

    1. The revival of modern *national* consciousness following the publication of Peretz Smolenskin's ETERNAL PEOPLE, Moses Hess's ROME AND JERUSALEM, Pinsker's

AUTO-EMANCIPATION and a number of other similar works.
2. The *social* idea that evolved as a consequence of the revolutions in France and America and the revolutionary movement in Russia.

A new conflict broke out between these two new ideas, which pushed the struggle between Hasidism and Haskalah into the backgrounds, and these two soon came to terms. Hasidism and Haskalah found their synthesis in the romantic neo-Hasidism of Peretz and his disciples, combined with their philosophical interpretations of Hillel Zeitlin, Martin Buber and others. At the same time, Moses Hess, Nachman Syrkin, Ber Borochov and their followers created the synthesis between nationalism and socialism. And, all these four ideas in Jewish life constituted a general synthesis of progressive Jewish thought, embracing—without any contradiction among themselves—Hasidism, Haskalah, nationalism, socialism, and finding complete expression in the reconstruction of the State of Israel.

This is a historical example of how it is possible and also necessary to draw strength from *all* the streams that have fertilized our national soil. It makes no difference that they once ran in contrary directions. All modern Jewish culture is and should be a sum total of all the forces that had previously combatted each other and afterwards were reconciled.

But this does not rule out differences of opinion in the context of ideas. There may be the ideological approach of one group of Jews who emphasize a special epoch in Jewish history, like the time when we Jews had our own State, or it may be the attitude of another group of Jews who lay stress on another period, such as that since our Dispersion.

But no one may say that only the period in which we had our own independent State is our entire history, any more than one may say that our whole history is only the period in which we lived in the Diaspora. The same holds for Territorialism. We must not confine our whole national life and endeavor to the limits of a Jewish land of our own, just as we must not stay content only with the opportunities of a distinctive Jewish life in the Diaspora.

The difference between Zionists and non-Zionists must not only be that one dismisses the Diaspora and the other minimizes our achievements in Israel. Israel is certainly of extraordinary importance to us, but we must at the same time bear in mind that even under the best conditions, the great mass of the Jewish people will remain in the Diaspora.

One may believe wholeheartedly with Achad Ha'am that out of Zion will come forth the Law, that the culture produced in the State of Israel will with its great achievements strengthen the power of the national resistance of the Jews in the Diaspora. Yet none of us may forget that we can and we must also be creative in the Dispersion.

Certainly the State of Israel is a bright spot in Jewish cultural and spiritual life. But all our achievements in Israel and all our latent possibilities concealed there are still a product of the material, spiritual and political forces we have accumulated in the Diaspora. All the pioneers of Israel, all its leaders came from the Diaspora to Israel, not the other way round. All the spiritual values we have there were not created in Israel, but were brought to Israel from the Diaspora.

Yet we are certainly justified in our belief that the deeper we become rooted in the cultural soil of Israel, the more fruitful will be the seed of our two thousand-year-old national world experience and the more the fruit growing in Israel will give taste and fragrance to the Jewish and the world seeds we have sown there.

Od lo ovdo tikvoteinu—we have a perfect faith that the People of Israel in the Land of Israel and the People of Israel in the Diaspora will never become thesis and antithesis, but will be and will not cease to be a wonderful synthesis which will maintain us on lofty spiritual heights, both on our own soil, in our own land, and in the Diaspora.

At the same time we must never lose our faith that in spite of all the harsh and bitter experiences we have had everywhere in the world, experiences that make a man, no matter how great his faith may be, become a doubter, in spite of the decline in world behavior, we must not lose our faith that ultimately man will regain his senses, and instead of pursuing the present road downhill to destruction, he will overcome the Satan concealed within him, and the light which is in him will dispel the darkness.

Messiah will come! He will come! Even though he tarry, he will come!

Rome, Jerusalem
and Nazareth

I. Ethical Aspects in Jewish Culture

*H*UMAN HORDES and tribes in the course of their wanderings over the surface of the globe quite naturally came in contact with one another. These encounters were not always of a pacific character: bloody clashes had been a frequent occurrence. These wars went on usually till one of the combatants gained the upper hand and subjugated his adversary. However, these gory clouds of war and destruction were not always without a silver lining in the form of a mutual understanding achieved at long last; and the enemies of yesterday learned to know one another at close range and gradually became friends, or contracted an alliance against a third party. Thus befriended, they eventually started on a course of intermarriage which led them in the long run to coalesce into one people. Tribes living as neighbors in proximity for a considerable length of time very seldom manage to keep out of a natural amalgamation. When a minority is planted in the midst of a majority it is almost next to impossible for it to show resistance enough to withstand the urge and the pressure brought to bear upon it by the majority group and not dissolve into the bigger body politic and cultural. Only three circumstances serve as a dam adequate to resist successfully the onrush of the assimilationist stream, or at any rate, to retard its flow.

Circumstance number one:

The minority constituting a ruling elite and being too proud to lose caste by interbreeding or hybridization of their racial stock. Such has been the attitude taken by most Europeans towards the natives in the colonial possessions controlled by them, or by the Hindus in their caste system.

Circumstance number two:

The minority being distinct from the majority through racial difference and being segregated and oppressed, humiliated by the superior majority. Such is the case of the three minorities found in the U.S.A., the dark, yellow, and red-skinned races. The minority under such circumstances is forced to lead an isolated life, to a certain extent, for it is sharply discriminated against. It is cordoned off, even when it is nourished by the same cultural diet to which it contributes its small pittance. Blacks are in no position to assimilate with the white-skinned majority, for the latter has taken preventive measures of a legalistic and extra-legalistic character against amalgamationist attempts. In various other countries mixed marriages between the white and dark are quite usual, but in the U.S.A. their number is insignificant. Often in the southern states, such couples ran the risk of being lynched.

Circumstance number three:

The respective cultures of the minority and the majority, though of a comparatively equal valuableness, having *sui generis* characteristics and basically divergent. Under such circumstances both parties are anxious to merge. This is in evidence among Hindus and Moslems in India; Christians and Moslems in Egypt, Syria and Lebanon; Armenians and Turks in Anatolia. This has also been the position occupied by the Jews in the past two thousand years of dispersion-life. We have lived in the midst of other peoples and yet led an isolated and insulated life, to quite a considerable measure. And not seldom was our segregation of our own choosing. There were periods in our checkered history when governmental pressure was brought upon us with the outspoken aim to fragmentize and dissolve us in the population among whom we dwelled. But we did not yield and readily suffered its punitive consequences. For sake of a complete assimilation with the majority we would have to discard our own cultural values and way of life, and this price we were not willing to pay.

Why did we refuse to mix with our neighbors constituting an overwhelming majority of the population? Why did we consider too exorbitant the price for the purchase of our freedom and riddance from persecution that quite often came dangerously near the point of annihilation?

THE MATERIALISTIC interpreters of history, such as the ones of the Marxian school, try to answer this question and account for this baffling phenomenon of non-assimilation in social-economic terms. The trouble with these elucidators of history is that they attempt to adjust historical occurrences to their *a priori* fixed and accepted theories rather than adjust the theories so that they should fit the events. A statement made by Karl Marx is with them something of Holy Writ truth, and no fact, no matter how stubborn and apparent, is allowed to contradict the Magister's dictum. It is a case of thesis exercising dictatorship over social nature. They will rather ignore the eye-opening fact or twist it out of shape altogether than change one iota or tittle in the Marxian Scripture. However, these Marxists are quite iconoclastic concerning all other dogmas but their own. On this point they are unusually fanatic and exceedingly bigoted. The great majority of the Jewish masses would no doubt have gained a great deal in the economic sense had they in the Middle Ages espoused the creed of the Church Triumphant. And the rich among the Jews would certainly have derived advantages of such an apostasy, as was shown actually by the few families who made no bones of crossing this religious Rubicon. And if the majority shunned this road they were not motivated in their refusal by sordid economic motives and materialistic considerations, but by *something* of a more idealistic nature.

This *something* was primarily the ethical and cultural national values which in their eyes have outweighed not only all the alluringly lucrative business prospects but even the worth of their biological lives in the literal meaning of the word. For an illustration let us take the Jewish population in Czarist Russia. They could have adopted the Greco-orthodox faith and thus with one stroke eliminated all the discriminatory laws that were in force against them, move out of their overcongested Pale, spread thinly all over the vast expanses of Russia, and in this way gain a free access to its almost limitless economic resources. They were offered this golden opportunity, but they rejected it with disdain, and preferred to stay as Jews in their over-crowded-to-suffocation ghetto. The Jews have unshakenly believed in the excellence and truthful significance of their own ethico-religious culture. But for this belief they would have long disappeared from the historical stage as a sociological entity. We laid so much stock by our *ethical* values that we Eastern European Jews, looked down upon the *political* values created by the European nations among whom we were compelled by our tragic destiny to live. We eschewed their political ways, shunned their mores and attitudes. Having such a negative relation to their *political* pattern we naturally could not have imitated them or envied their more fortunate lot. Our respective outlooks could not mix. They were so different. And to establish a *modus vivendi* was quite a difficult task. So that the only road that remained open to us was the Via Dolorosa. And we followed this road of sufferings and humiliation with utmost dignity and internal pride, with uplifted heads and eyes fixed on the stars of redemption twinkling to us with solace of promise from the remote future. And the darker and gloomier the night of our lives became, the brighter our stars of hope shone.

What I am driving at is virtually not more than to state again with special emphasis the fact that we Jews are an ethical nation par excellence, i.e., in possession of a specific ethico-religious culture that is distinct from the secular political culture of the European peoples, and this distinction is of such a magnitude and import, that those among us who were endowed with a strong will power and a keen sense for spiritual values were ready to go through torture and ruin rather than abandon these treasures. We did no bargaining and wanted no compromises.

This characteristic of Jewish culture was boldly shown from the very start of Israel's ethical development, in the spiritual conflict between Rome and Jerusalem.

THE CONFLICTS between Rome and Jerusalem were embittered and merciless. For these two were situated at diametrically opposite poles. As symbols representing two definite world-outlooks, Jerusalem is the light of the world, and Rome its darkness.

Rome laid the cornerstone for the edifice of a political civilization which has proved to be so brutal and inhumanly cruel that it again threatens to end in a world-catastrophe, in a total collapse not only of organized society but of the human race as a whole. Jerusalem nursed and nourished the religious and ethical values of Judaism as well as its Christian offshoot. Together they are at the present time the only positive factors that still have a chance to arrest the destructive march of historical events towards extinction of all human achievements and even of the very existence of mankind on this not too hospitable planet.

Anthropologically speaking, hardly a vestige remains of the ancient Romans. The so-called Latin peoples that live in or around the areas once occupied by the Roman Empire are not direct descendants of the Roman stock. They are an admixture of various tribes and diverse strands which in their peregrinations crossed and sometimes settled in the provinces that were the witnesses of the grandeur that *was* Rome.

As regards modern Jews, some contend, and maybe correctly, that in our veins alien blood-streams flow. This in itself is not of paramount importance. Essential for us is not our consanguinity but our cultural affinity. Contemporary Jews are spiritually as far removed from Rome and its civilizational legacy as the ancient Jews were.

In quiet, peaceful periods there was no urgent need to examine these circumstances. Little thought was given to the intransigence existing between Roman civilization and Jewish ethical religious culture. Because of our failure to stress these differences a number of Jews, after the epoch of Emancipation and Enlightenment, became fascinated by the external gloss and glitter of the Roman European civilization and showed a willingness to make concessions to it or to part with their Jewishness altogether. But our time is a critical one. The threat of a new world war hangs over our heads as a Damoclean sword of immense proportions. With one stroke it may cut the throat of humankind, thus realize the cherished wish of Caligula. Jews, as was always the case in history, receive the lion's share of the common sufferings of the human race. In World War II we lost over a third of our people in the inhuman massacres organized by Hitler and his satanic henchmen. After surviving such an experience it is quite natural that we should evaluate critically the ideologies and outlooks that led up to a catastrophe of such unprecedented magnitude and such tragic tenor. Together with the Jews a number of serious-minded Christians are now ready to shake from their feet the glittering dust of Rome or, more correctly, of Romanism, i.e., what ancient Rome stood for basically.

II. ROME

THE ESSENCE of Rome is political power, might above all considerations of right; might which replaces right to all intents and purposes. He who has the strength to impose his will can never go wrong, for wrong is embedded in weakness. None judges the victor, for he is the provisional and historical judge, and his judgment is enduring so long as his victory is stabilized. Rome knows of no other criterion of Justice. Success by its very results always and invariably justifies itself pragmatically. Conquest, meaning seizure, is the source of all possessional privileges and prerogatives. The acknowledged Jewish-Christian concept of righteousness and equity as being an autonomous category is for Rome an absurdity. For the spoils belong to the victor and he has the unlimited right to enjoy them in no lesser measure than the lion devouring his quarry. Rome not only legalizes the enslavement of its war captives but also allows itself to spill their innocent blood for the sake of mere amusement, forcing them to duel ferocious beasts in the arena for the enjoyment of spectators who are delighted by the sight of the captives writhing in agony between the jaws and claws of tigers or lions. According to Roman concepts, nothing prejudicial, let alone shocking to human conscience, results from these atrocious arrangements. Rome is devoid of sentimentalism and knows no sympathy or mercy. War, according to its lights, is a noble and lofty pursuit, soldierism is an ideal institution, and a warrior must not be a weakling. Mercy is a sign of ignoble weakness, debility, unbecoming a virtuous (which is synonymous with virile) man. Upon these basic principles Roman law is founded; and this body of law, the Justinian Code, served as a foundation for European legislation.

"The systematized body of Roman law, made by order of the Emperor Justinian in the sixth century... has furnished the material for, or largely shaped, the law of the modern civilized world."[1] According to Rome, there is no such thing as social justice. Ownership is enclosed within power, abides in force to make one's claim stand, well defended. "... But property is conditioned by might. What I have in my power, that is my own... Thus property and possession coincide... It is not a right lying outside my might that legitimizes me, but solely my might."[2] Hence inequality, the division of society into servants and masters, patricians and plebeians; in short, the split into masses and classes, ruled and rulers, governed and governors. Hence our present day, as well as age-old, social iniquity and all its evil derivatives that keep on convulsing and shaking society to its very foundations and from time to time drench it with blood and consume it in flames of internecine wars.

Rome was highly successful militarily and politically. By far the greatest part of the then-known and civilized world was subjugated by it. True, Rome granted the conquered provinces and countries some form of limited home-rule. It left, almost intact, their ways of life, their folk-habits, customs, cults and standards of intercourse. It interfered not too much with their modes of worship; the local political machinery was left in the hands of native rulers, and their religious status quo ante was maintained by their priests, undisturbed to a certain degree. Rome felt satisfied with exercising sovereignty and supervision over all these activities so as to be assured that the regnant kings and officiating clergy were loyal to Rome, ready to do its bidding in any emergency, and what was of first interest, would keep a watchful eye on the submerged masses lest they rise in rebellion and attempt to shake off the yoke of Rome. Some form of a partnership was constituted between the foreign and the native despoilers. The local satraps, temporal as well as "spiritual," played the game of Rome, robbing and plundering the populace and dividing the spoils. In recompense Rome was always ready to defend them against any outburst of a rebellious character by the downtrodden masses threatening the established regime. The conditions of life of the lowly under the cruel domination of Rome were unbearable. They were reduced to a status resembling that of beasts of burden. They were pariahs economically and politically.

The power of Rome was concentrated mainly in its legions, its glorious army. On the upkeep of its armed forces Rome spent abundantly. The army was well provided, lavishly fed and extravagantly clothed in comparison with other national militias. In spite of the excessive expenditures the army was a paying proposition, a profitable concern. The colossal outlay gave handsome returns. The Roman legions marched from victory to victory, captured one country after another. A swollen stream of looted riches kept on flowing to Rome incessantly. The subjugated peoples were bled white, made to live in a state of semi, or full starvation, while Rome bathed in luxury. Rome became a cesspool of vice and corruption. All variants of sexual licentiousness and perversion were practiced and even flaunted publicly as virtues to take pride in. Fabulous wealth was spent in debaucheries. To replenish the emptied coffers of the public treasury, military expeditions were organized and sent off in all haste to plunder the neighboring peoples. And when the neighboring lands had been picked clean, Rome dispatched its army into farther lands and into more remote provinces.

Slavery in that era was a common practice, a legitimized institution. Various states waged wars against each other and the prisoners used to be brought by the victors back to the homeland or sold into slavery in the markets of foreign lands. But none abused this damned practice to such a large measure as the Roman Empire. It quite often conducted wars with the sole purpose of capturing prisoners, thus having at its disposal cheap labor. In the wake of its legions a multitude of slave-dealers followed. The traffic in human beings went on right on the battlefields. These wars resembled hunting parties. Where there were prospects of getting slaves of a better quality, thereto the Roman expeditions were lured. Cicero shamelessly contended that it did not pay to make war in Britain, for the slaves imported therefrom were of a low grade, hardly worth their salt. He pointed out that it was more advantageous to wage war in Greece where the human element of both sexes stood on a higher level both of physical and of mental development and therefore made slaves of a better physique, stronger endurance and higher intelligence.

The Romans divided the human race in two classes. They, the Romans, belonged to the elite, to the first pick of humanity, the rest of the inhabitants of the earth were rated low, as almost subhuman. They existed on sufferance, their function was to serve the master-people, to be drones and drudges and thus give the Roman aristocracy the possibility to enjoy its leisure and spend its time in idleness and extravagance, seeking pleasure and gratifying its highly refined and extremely titillated appetites.

Slaves did not come under the common human denominator. They were classified as vocal instruments. The grading ran as follows: articulate instruments—slaves; semi-articulate—oxen, beasts of burden or draught; inarticulate—plain tools. Horses were rated far above this triple line, for they were the motive force of the chariots, and thus made themselves useful in the pursuit of war.

Two-thirds of the Roman population was made up of slaves. They did all the work in the fields as well as the households. Not only did they serve their exacting masters but even entertained them. The most favorable form of diversion for the Romans was the spectacle of fights and bloodshed. The well-built and muscular slaves were trained to be gladiators and were usually killed in the amphitheaters. Even female slaves were trained as gladiatrixes. Their task was to fight with dwarfs. Women-slaves were the personal property of their Roman masters and were used by them for the gratification of sexual lust. When they grew tired of them they sold them as arena-fodder. For a slave, male or female, killed accidentally or murdered in cold blood by a Roman, the fine exacted by the law was no more than approximately three dollars in U.S.A. legal tender. This was their pecuniary rating.[3]

III. JERUSALEM

ROME WAS the thesis of the ancient world, Jerusalem its antithesis. Against the Roman principle of might above all, Jerusalem proclaimed justice above all and everything. Rome taught that the drawn sword is the arbiter and dispenser of all earthly goods; in opposition to this, Jerusalem asserted that man's property was a gift of God and it could be rightly acquired only through righteous deeds. "... For thy and thine is His, for thus David says: 'For of Thee comes all and of Thine we have given Thee.'" (I. Chron. XXIX, 14)[4] Jerusalem's maxim of conduct was: "Do not to your fellow-man what you don't want him to do to you."[5] This is the golden rule expressed in negative terms.[6] Rome could not comprehend such a strange rule of conduct. According to Roman conception one was allowed to do anything to one's fellow-man if only one derived from his action pleasure or profit, for the interests of men always clash, are found at cross-purposes, and people should take advantage one of the other. Jerusalem taught that a man reached a high degree of development in the moral sense which alone counted when he applied the following rule: "Mine is yours, and yours is yours."[7] Rome taught the very reverse: "What is thine is mine, and mine is surely mine." Aboth classifies it as the rule of the wicked.[8] In the code of the ancient Hebrews there are a number of restrictive measures to be applied against the abuses of the wealthy and mighty ones in the land. These are means to curb their acquisitive appetites and their inclinations to oppress economically the unfavored masses, the weak links in the chain of social intercourse. The Prophets were not only divinely inspired teachers of pure and refined religion, but also leaders of the lowly in their struggle against the tyranny of the ruler and despotism of the money-aristocracy. They were fearless fighters for social justice. Their word was like a flame burning with indignation and they paid with their lives for the cause of social righteousness. The father of the Prophets, the divine lawgiver Moses, is according to Holy Scripture, also the leader and liberator of the enslaved Israelites. The Lord appeared unto him and said: "I have surely seen the affliction of my people which are in Egypt, and have heard their cry by reason of their taskmasters; for I know their sorrows."[9]

What a strange and peculiar ring a pronouncement of this kind must have had for the Roman ear! The Almighty considers the slaves, who are deprived even of souls. He takes interest in their miserable lot, listens to their wretched complaints, hears their cry for justice being denied them! Such a behavior would be unbecoming any ordinary master, the more so the Master of all masters, the King of all kings. Why, such a weakness shown by a ruler would be branded as unworthy of his position, as almost criminal, offensive. And if the Lord acts in such a despicable way, what kind of a God is he anyway! His conduct is utterly undignified, condemnable.

However, according to the Jewish comprehension this act was the true mark of the genuine dignity of the Almighty. God is the protector of the poor. He is their self-appointed guardian. "He dwells with the oppressed and the humble of spirit."[10] And His voice is not with the vulgar and noisy, the boisterous and ostentatious. He does not side with the mighty and successful, those who storm and bring down the strongholds of their enemies, not with those who shake the earth with the chatter of the charges of their victorious equestrian legions. He is with the ne'er-do-wells, with the broken and bruised reeds of the social silva.

"Now behold, the Lord was passing by, and a great and mighty wind was rending the mountain and shattering the rocks before God; but God was not in the wind... but in the sound of a still small voice." [11]

The forte of the weak and the wronged is their consciousness of being right and suffering for a just cause. Moses was a leader of revolting slaves, and the revolt was crowned with complete success. The weak and meek, the unarmed slaves, whose might is their right to liberty, overcame the mighty Pharaoh with his hosts and chariots and thus they broke the chains of their serfdom.

The basis of the Mosaic code composed by a liberator of slaves was, quite naturally, justice, protection of the needy and oppressed.

The farmer in straitened circumstances could lease out his holdings, but nobody could buy them in perpetuity, for the land belonged to God.[12] Once in fifty years a jubilee was declared and all the lands acquired through purchase were returned to their original owners. The same law was applicable to the sold village-houses.[13] This periodical redistribution was a preventive measure against driving the poor farmers off their small lots by the circumventing, scheming, crafty rich.

The have's were commanded to give charity to the have-not's. "If there be among you a poor man of one of your brethren within any of your gates... you shall open your hands wide unto him. For the poor shall never cease out of the land, therefore, I command you, saying, you shall open your hands wide unto your brother, to your poor and to your needy in your land."[14] No interest on loans was permitted.[15] Even a pledge given as collateral to secure the payment of the loan was not permitted to be held in case the pledgee was in need of it for his personal use. "When you do lend your brother anything, you shall not go into his house to fetch his pledge. You shall stand abroad, and the man to whom you lend shall bring out the pledge abroad unto you. And if the man be poor, you shall not sleep with his pledge. In any case you shall deliver him the pledge again when the sun goes down, that he may sleep in his raiment, and bless you and it shall be righteous unto you before God your Elohim."[16] The relations between the employer and employee were regulated so as to protect the hired worker against possible abuse at the hand of his hirer. "You shall not oppress a hired servant that is poor and needy, whether he be of your brethren or of your strangers that are in your land within your gates. At his day you shall give him his hire, neither shall the sun go down upon it; for he is poor and is expecting his wages."[17] The status of strangers was established juridically so that they might not fall victims of xenophobia and be persecuted. "Love you, therefore, the stranger, for you were strangers in the land of Egypt."[18] The foundation of the shortened work-week was laid down firmly and broadly in the commandment to rest on the seventh day. "But the seventh day is the Sabbath... in it thou shalt not do any work... that thy manservant and thy maidservant may rest as well as thou. And remember that thou wast a servant in the land of Egypt... therefore God thy Elohim commanded thee to keep the Sabbath day."[19]

Slavery was not abolished outright, for at that time it would have been too radical a step (we must not forget that slavery in many countries of Europe and even in the U.S.A. was abolished some three thousand years later), but it was curtailed and mitigated to a degree that made it lose its basic characteristics;[20] it became limited in time, reduced to a period of six years and no longer.[21] "For unto me the children of Israel are servants; they are my servants,"[22] "and not servants of servants."[23] When he is freeing his manservant the master is commanded to provide him with ample means to make it easier for the ex-slave to settle and start life economically on his own. "And when you send him out free, you shall not let him go away empty. You shall furnish him liberally out of your flock, and out of your winepress; of that wherewith God your Elohim has blessed you, you shall give unto him."[24] Fugitive slaves were not returned to their masters. "You shall not deliver unto his master the servant which is escaped from his master unto you. He shall dwell with you, even among you, in that place which he shall choose in one of your gates, where it likes him best: you shall not oppress him."[25] Women-slaves, in cases where their master had sexual intercourse with them, were given a status equal to that of legally taken wives, and they could not be dismissed without the due process of divorce.[26] The children of the maid-servants were legitimate children entitled to all the rights and privileges enjoyed by the offspring of the wives taken in formal wedlock.[27]

Hebrew legislation being based on ethical foundation is characterized by its interest in safeguarding the welfare of the afflicted, the socially handicapped, such as widows, orphans and other underprivileged.[28]

This human outlook found its reflection not only in legislative enactments but in Jewish folklore as well. The inhabitants of the earth were destroyed by a deluge as a punishment for their immoral behavior.[29] Sodom and Gommorah

were burned and overthrown as a visitation for their inhos-
pitality, vice and corruption.[30] The Book of Psalms, a collection of edifying lyrics, is rightly considered the classic hym-
nal of all the forsaken, mistreated by men and wronged by
destiny.[31] For a key to this great work the following verse
can serve: "Turn unto me and have mercy upon me, for I
am lonely and afflicted."[32]

IV. NAZARETH

BOTH PARENTS of Yeshu of Nazareth (Jesus) were Jewish.[33] He
was born and raised in a Jewish environment in accordance
with Jewish tradition.[34] In his short life he inaugurated no
new religion and he had no mind to do anything of the kind.
He came not to destroy the Law, but to fulfill it.[35] He called
himself "Son of man,"[36] a designation profusely used by the
prophet Ezekiel.[37] He apostrophized the Creator "Father,"[38]
not because he laid claim to a special filiation grounded in a
supernatural mode of birth, but simply because this was the
accepted form of addressing the Almighty, blessed be He, in
Jewish prayers. He called the Holy One "my Father,"[39] but
he also used the expression "thy Father,"[40] "your Father,"[41]
and "our Father."[42] His disciples and close followers were
all of them Jews.[43] The movement inspired and spiritually
guided by him was exclusively Jewish.[44] "I am not sent but
unto the lost sheep of the House of Israel."[45] "These twelve
Jesus sent forth, and commanded them, saying, Go not into
the way of the Gentiles, and into *any* city of the Samaritans
enter ye not."[46]

Jesus actually followed in the footsteps of the Prophets.
He represented an organic growth of Judaism. The true
meaning of Judaism as an ethical way of life he spread
among the broad masses,[47] the so-called or nicknamed
"people of the earth." He endeavored to instill in them a
sense of dignity. He wanted to uplift them spiritually and

socially. He taught them the doctrine of love[48] and coopera-
tion,[49] and above all peace.[50]

In his conduct, as well as in his teaching, one thing is
shown clearly, and that is he sided with the laboring and
hard-working masses. He tried to lighten their burden of
ignorance and poverty.[51] He opposed the rich,[52] who were in
his time, as in most other times, morally corrupt and degenerated, Hellenized to the point of forsaking all Jewish cultural values and despising the masses.

The Pharisees whom he stigmatized as hypocrites[53] are
not the Pharisees, the founders of the Talmud, but a deca-
dent fringe of the Hellenized intellectuals and arrogant aristocrats.

"Those Pharisees whom Jesus reviles and reproaches, the
Talmud likewise condemns. And here we shall adduce the
evidence for our statement. The Pharisees censored Jesus
for his healing on the Sabbath day (Luke, VI, 6-11), and the
Pharisees, the composers of the Talmud, allowed healing on
Sabbath (Yoma 85b). This is still more remarkable, for Jesus
uses the Talmudic argument, 'If a man on the Sabbath day
receives circumcision, that the law of Moses should not be
broken; are ye angry at me because I have made a man
every whit whole on the Sabbath day' (John, VII, 23).

"Jesus justified the action of His disciples: 'The Sabbath
was made for man, and not man for the Sabbath. Therefore
the Son of Man is Lord also of the Sabbath' (Mark, II, 27-28).
An equivalent expression is used by the fathers of the Talmud: 'Sabbath is given to you, and not you to Sabbath'
(Yoma, 85b).

"Jesus expostulates with the Pharisees: 'Have ye never
read what David did, when he had need, and was hungered,
he and they that were with him? How he went into the
house of God in the days of Abiathar the high priest, and
did eat the showbread, which is not lawful to eat but for the
priests, and gave also to them which were with him? (Mark,

II, 25-26). This very argument is used by the Talmud (Mena-
choth, 95b; Yoma 83a, Jerus. Yoma, ch. VIII, 5) to prove that a
man tantalized by hunger is allowed to eat any kind of food
disregarding the dietary laws and the sanctity of Sabbath as
well, and it bases its decision on that very verse quoted by
Jesus.

"Concerning vows: 'Woe unto you, ye blind guides,
which say, Whosoever shall swear by the temple, it is nothing; but whosoever shall swear by the gold of the temple, he
is a debtor! Ye fools and blind: for whether is greater, the
gold or the temple that sanctifieth the gold? And, Whosoever shall swear by the altar, it is nothing; but whosoever
sweareth by the gift that is upon it, he is guilty. Ye fools and
blind: for whether is greater, the gift or the altar that sanctifieth the gift?' (Matthew, XXIII, 16-19). This very opinion is
held by the fathers of the Talmud. (Nedarim 10b) 'Who
swears by the temple, by the altar is under obligation to
keep his vow.'

"'And he that shall swear by heaven, sweareth by the
throne of God, and by Him that sitteth thereon' (Matthew,
XXIII, 22). The identical stand is taken by the Talmud (Sha-
buoth, 35a; Yore Deah, 237; Chokmath Adam, LXXXIX, 11).

"Consequently the Pharisees that Jesus criticized so
harshly could not be those of the Talmud, called by us
Perushim."[54]

I neither pose nor intend to answer the question whether
Jesus was right or wrong. All I want to do is to point out
that Jesus, according to the portrayal given of him in the
Gospels, did not deviate from the traditional ways of
Judaism. He accepted its basic doctrine and scrupulously
observed its practices. He obviously was at variance with
some of the spiritual leaders and spokesmen of Jewry of his
time, but his disagreement was not of a broader gauge and
deflection from the common stream than the divergence
existing between the school of Hillel and that of Shamai.

And all these disputations and debates took place within a closely knit Jewish environment, and they revolved around points in interpretation of the Mosaic law and forms and manners of their application. Jesus in his time was not less a genuinely Jewish personality and indigenous phenomenon of Jewish cultural life than the rest of the sages and scribes, the teachers and commentators of divine law. The Sadducees and the aristocracy were assimilated; they adopted foreign modes of thinking, and living. Not so Jesus and his disciples. They were homogeneous, pious, observant Jews.[55]

It is commonly accepted that Saul of Tarsus, known under the name of Paul the Apostle to the Gentiles, is to carry the burden of blame for the split between Judaism and Christianity. True enough, Paul aroused the anger of the sages because he abolished the observance of circumcision, the dietary laws, the strictures concerning the keeping of holidays, and dared to interpret the Holy Writ in his own original way. Of him it is written in Aboth: "He who profanes the sancta, and despises the festivals, and makes void the covenant of our father, Abraham, and construes the Holy Scripture not in accordance with the established rules of the sages, even though he be possessed of learning and good deeds, he has no portion in the world to come."[56] It is interesting to note that even his bitterest antagonists, the fathers of the Talmud, considered Paul a scholar and a man of exemplary conduct. They do not brand him as a traitor or an apostate. Not only Jesus, even Paul had no intention to break away from Judaism altogether and create a new religion; all he wanted was to give traditional Judaism a new direction. He and his associates still kept within the sphere of the Mosaic law. He called himself "a Pharisee the son of a Pharisee."[57] He testified of his life: "... After the most straightest sect of our religion I lived a Pharisee."[58] He and those who shared his views were looked upon as one of the splinter sects Jewry abounded in at that epoch of political unrest and spiritual fermentation.

Not only in the circles of the Pharisees was Paul severely criticized and condemned; even the true followers of Jesus censored him sharply.[59] Some went as far as to spread false rumors about him, starting a whispering campaign denying his Jewish extraction. They alleged him to be a Greek who had embraced Judaism for ulterior motives, not out of conviction, but because of his wooing the daughter of a Jewish priest. Being rejected by the fair maiden, he took off his disguise and began crusading against circumcision and other observances prescribed by Mosaic law.

We repeat our basic thesis: neither Jesus nor the apostles abandoned traditional Judaism and parted with the Jewish mores. They lived like Orthodox Jews, and died like Jewish martyrs. The schism between the Messianist and the true-to-the-letter-of-the-law Jews occurred at a much later date. The split took place when Rome embraced Christianity and did it on its own terms. It accepted only the Judeo-Christian mythology, the external form of the creed, but not its internal moral content. Instead of adjusting its political and economic life to the salvationist doctrine of the Kingdom of Heaven, as it should have done in all earnest and truth, Rome adjusted the teaching of Redemption to its political notions and economic practices which were deeply rooted in pagan iniquity. Rome emasculated the Messianistic teaching, flattened out the extreme demands of true Christianity. In reality it was not Rome which espoused Christianity, but the very reverse took place, Christianity espoused Romanism.

Radical Christianity capitulated before this secular pagan imperialist great power. Christianity in this new atavism became estranged of Judaism. Christianity was depleted of its ethical substance, turned its back upon its extreme moralism, discarded its lofty idealism and made its peace with Roman imperialist politics. In this metamorphosis it was embodied in a Triumphant Ecclesiasticism that bought its triumph for the price of a full-measured opportunism.

Christianity shared the fate of its great leader and inspirer: it was crucified by the Romans. The first crucifixion they carried out in their capacity of outspoken enemies, the second they executed in their capacity of allegedly avowed friends, "wolves in sheeps' clothing." And the vision of the Emperor Constantine was truly symbolic. In *hoc signo vinces*, pagan Rome won and Jewish Nazareth lost the battle.

REFERENCES

1. Funk and Wagnall's *New Standard Dictionary*, art. Code.
2. Max Stirner, *The Ego and his Own*, p. 332, New York, 1915.
3. Mommsen, *History of Rome*, vol. II, p.76—E. Gibbon, *Decline and Fall of the Roman Empire*, vol. 1, pp. 39-42, 1925.
4. Aboth, III, 8.
5. Shabbath, 31a.
6. Matthew, VII, 12.
7. Aboth, V, 13.
8. Ibid.
9. Exodus, III, 7.
10. Isaiah, LVII, 15.
11. I. Kings, XIX, 12.
12. Leviticus, XXV, 23.
13. Ibid., 28-31.
14. Deuteronomy, XV, 7-11.
15. Exodus, XXII, 25; Leviticus, XXV, 36; Deut., XII, 20.
16. Deut., XXIV, 10-13.
17. Ibid., X, 19; Ex., XXII, 20; XXIII, 9.
18. Exodus, XXIII, 9.
19. Deut., V, 14-15; Lev., XIX, 33; Ex., XXIII, 12.
20. Kiddushin, 20a.
21. Ex., XXI, 2-6.
22. Lev., XXV, 55.
23. Kiddushim, 22b.
24. Deut., XV, 14.
25. Ibid., XXIII, 16-17.
26. Ibid., XXI, 10-14; Ex., XXI, 7-9.
27. Genesis, XXX.
28. Deut., XXIV, 17; Ex., XXII, 21.
29. Gen., VI, 5-7
30. Ibid., XVIII, 20-24.
31. Psalms, X, 14, 18; LXVIII, 6, LXXXII, 3. CXLVI, 9.
32. Ibid., XXV, 16.
33. Matthew, I, 18.
34. Luke, II, 21-24; 27; 49.

35. Mat., V, 17-18.
36. Ibid., IX, 6; X, 23; II, 19; 13, 37, 41, and numerous other places
37. Ezekiel, through all the book.
38. Mat., II, 25.
39. Ibid., XVIII, 10; XXVI, 29; XIII, 50, and numerous other places.
40. Ibid., VI, 18.
41. Ibid., V, 16, 45, 48; VI, 8, 18, 26.
42. Ibid., VI, 19.
43. Ibid., X, 2-5; Mark, III, 15-19.
44. Mat., XIX, 28; Luke, XXII, 30; Acts, VI, 7.
45. Mat., XV, 24.
46. Ibid., X, 5.
47. Ibid., XI, 5.
48. Ibid., VII, 12; John, XIII, 35-36.
49. John, X, 16.
50. Mat., V, 24-26.
51. Ibid., XI, 28.
52. Ibid., XIX, 23-24; Luke, XVIII, 25.
53. Mat., XXIII, 13-15; 23; 27; 29.
54. Rabbi L. M. Gordin, *What is the Talmud?* pp. 6-10, Vilno, 1909 (Russian)
55. Mark, I, 44; Mat., XXIII, 3.
56. Aboth, III, 15.
57. Acts, XXIII, 6.
58. Ibid., XXVI, 5.
59. Ibid., XV, 2.

INTRODUCTION
TO KABBALA

$\mathscr{A}$LBERT EINSTEIN, who penetrated deeper than anyone
to the mysteries of nature, devoted his genius for the last
irty years of his life to determining whether there is cos-
ic harmony in the universe. He broke down the traditional
irrier between matter and energy, which had been erected
ɩ the science of physics, and he showed that though there
e two different expressions of the integral structure of
hich the world is built, essentially they are one.

He also made it clear that what is most vast in the cos-
os and what is least, the tiniest, are both subject to one and
e same law. He established the theory that radiation, grav-
ɩtion, magnetism and all that is concerned with them, up
ɩ the composition of the countless billions of constellations,
ɩch consisting of countless billions of stars, planets, com-
s, down to the smallest cells of which living bodies are
ɩnstituted, are all directed by one single natural law, and
ɩe subject to one single mysterious *Will*.

Centuries before Einstein, long before modern times,
abbala had in its development and its ramifications shown
ɩecisely that, in a figurative, metaphorical sense. Kabbala
ɩd already come to the conclusion that all that exists in the
ɩsmos arose from one single *Will*, and behaves according

to the established laws of that one single *Will*. With this difference—Einstein directed his attention to the physical world, while the Kabbala included in its theory the spiritual world as well as the physical. Kabbala combined intellectual consciousness with physical existence, and from the synthesis created a unity—to this extent, that *everything originates from one source,* and that one and the same *Will* governs everything.

How did Einstein formulate and explain his scientific theories? By using mathematical formulas expressed in symbols, letters of the alphabet, numerals, and mathematical equations. For instance, his well-known formula which led to the discovery of the hidden power concealed in the atom, and formulated thus: E-energy = M-mass (mass being the totality of matter) multiplied by the velocity of light (186,000 miles a second) squared ($E=MC^2$).

Obviously these Einsteinian mathematical formulas, so convincing that they could bring about the revolution they caused in physics, were not reached easily, or reached through some sudden inspiration. They were arrived at after years and years of research and observation by Einstein himself and through the scientific investigations of the greatest physicists over generations. Einstein's genius was all-embracing. He questioned many earlier scientific theories, and came to his own theoretical conclusions, whose results he explained through his unique mathematical formulas.

The Kabbalists employed similar methods. They took into account the different faiths and teachings of the world, the researches, suppositions, hypotheses and considerations of original thinkers and of the folk masses of all nations. With all this in mind they developed their own belief, and in order to explain it they too used mathematical formulas.

The only difference between the two sets of formulas—the scientific and the speculative Kabbalist—is this: the scientific explanations used Roman letters and Arabic numerals, while the Kabbalists used Hebrew letters and Hebrew numerals. The method is similar, though the symbols are different.

Of course, there is a fundamental difference between Kabbala and science. Science is based on experience and Kabbala on faith. But the more science reveals of nature, the more nature remains concealed from it. Modern science can achieve a great deal *technically* but there is a big difference between being able to *use* things and *knowing* what these things *are.*

Science still doesn't know what light is—whether it is composed of particles, according to the Quantum theory, or of waves, or of both. Science has indeed discovered that matter and energy are but two parts of the same thing, but it has not the slightest conception yet of what this thing *is.* Science doesn't know what gravity is, or electro-magnetism. The more science reveals, the more nature which encircles us grows mysterious and concealed.

We are still troubled by the question of all questions— what is *existence* and *why*? Why are we born and why do we die? What is the purpose of this whole process? What is the purpose of all the sufferings man endures from the cradle to the grave? Science can give no answer.

Kabbala does try to answer all these questions. Not the question of the physical composition of matter. That is not its concern. But it does try to explain the *Will* that brought matter and man into existence—to explain the overall sublime energy that creates the energy to create matter.

Certainly, the theses advanced by Kabbala cannot be proved empirically—at least not in every regard. But the Kabbalists assume—rightly perhaps—that what impels human reason and gives it the possibility of seeing over and beyond the boundaries of the senses are the best, the most wonderful and truest tools for arriving at the truth, incomparably superior to any mechanical instruments.

What is the world, the Kabbalists conclude, if it is not to be found within the bounds of human cognition? And if human thought recognizes a nature that goes over and beyond the limits of experience and of the physical senses—recognizes a higher world that is perceived by spiritual senses, a world to which our physical world is only relative—who can say that this thought and visionary world is not true?

And if this thought and vision-conceived and recognized truth is capable of filling human minds to the pitch of immense enthusiasm, of ecstasy, of boundless bliss, praise be! Blessed be everything that can transport the human mind from a sense of hell to a sense of paradise, that releases man's thought from pain.

To FORMULATE the essential of all essentials Kabbala uses three letters—Yod, Hay, Vov—the Hay twice. The formula is explained thus:

Yod—wisdom, the attribute of father, united (for the purpose of creation) with Hay-Bina, the attribute of mother. That is Father-Mother—the essential of all essentials, the higher world. This unison gave birth to Vov, and Vov is the son of Yod-Hay—the lower world. Thus the creation was consummated. This is expressed in one of the Symbols of the Divine, the Shem-Haviah.

This is the essential of all essentials, and all things else are but commentary and the result of this origin.

The higher world is the world of *Spirit*, whose existence people recognize only through pure reason. The lower world is the world of *Matter*, the physical world, which people recognize through the senses.

KABBALA is a way of thought whose origin goes back to the very beginning of consciousness. It is the concentration, the absolute, most refined crystallization of the experiences, thoughts and revelations that have come to people with exceptional depth of sensitiveness in the evolution of the mystical trend of thought has has gripped the mind of man since his primitive state, and has developed his religious feelings and his philosophic standpoint from the origin to the most advanced and cultivated contemporary religions.

That original thought of man contained the embryo, the germ from which Kabbala developed. From that source it grew and branched out to become the modern thought of man, which strives to explain the essence and the meaning of *Being.*

Our entire physical world, including man, as far as it is perceived through the senses, is based on three foundations which are simultaneously great mysteries—*Birth, Life, Death.*

How and by what means does birth come about? Biologically it is explained as the result of the fertilization of the feminine by the masculine. But when we probe the matter deeper, this explanation will not satisfy. It opens up many new questions. Why is fertilization needed? And if it is needed, how and why does it produce a creature of the same shape and form as the fertilizer and the fertilized? And other similar questions concerning the essence of *Being.*

Other difficult questions arise in connection with *Existence.* How do things perpetuate themselves? Why? Why are there different species among living creatures when their physical qualities are so similar? Why are there different vegetations when fundamentally they are the same? Why does one tree produce apples and another pears or plums or nuts when their roots all draw nourishment from the same soil?

So too with *Death.* Why? What is its sense and purpose? How?

Human knowledge has not yet found the answer to these questions. Science has indeed made great advances in all fields, has uncovered many mysteries, but it has touched only the surface. It has not penetrated to the depths. Science does not even hope to be able to reveal the essence of *Being*, the mystery of *Becoming*, the *How*. And it certainly does not consider it within the bounds of its experiences to delve into the essential of all essentials—*How, Why* and for *What Purpose* all this?

All these questions which the advanced man today asks were already asked by the original man as soon as he emerged from the animal state and, as the Bible tells us, ate the fruit of the Tree of Knowledge of good and evil. He saw various natural phenomena which were riddles to him. He was filled with wonder at all the contradictions in nature—life and death, light and shadow, day and night, summer and winter and so forth. Some natural phenomena gave him pleasure, others pain.

Then he posed deeper questions—what creates in man the two contrary emotions, joy and pain? What is their meaning? Why, for what purpose have they been planted in man? Man realized that there are strange, unknown, invisible powers that cause all these mysterious happenings, that govern him and all surrounding nature. From this realization he gradually evolved his religious ideas.

The first religious philosophies were naturally as primitive as primitive man. Man conceived of all kinds of gods, good and bad, who governed good and bad natural phenomena. He worshiped them, elaborated rituals for their worship, prayed to them, and brought them sacrifices.

As man developed, his religious conceptions also developed, became more philosophical, profounder, so that the later religious cults, like those of the Near East—Babylon, Egypt, Greece—and of the Orient—India, China—stood on a very high level. But none of these peoples reached the conception of the Unity of Creation, of the One, the Only God, the Sole Cause of All Causes; *He* is the Creator of the Universe, and its Ruler, in accordance with His own established, everlasting unitary laws. This is the conception of the Unity of Creation, to which the authors of the Kabbala, which means the Jewish People, rose.

Of course, in its beginnings Kabbala, too, was primitive. But it progressed and evolved, and in time it arrived at man's modern thought. In other words, Kabbala incorporates the entire history of human intellectual development— from the primitive to the latest discoveries of Science. For example:

Kabbala presumes that everything in the physical world is only an expression of the *higher* world, which is not physical. Modern science has reached the same conclusions, though it expresses them in different terms. Modern scientific research has confirmed the idea that Einstein first evolved, that matter and energy are not two different substances, but are directly derived from each other. In other words, matter is nothing other than concentrated energy.

What is energy? The scientists answer that it is one of nature's greatest mysteries. The more science investigates it, the more mysterious it becomes. Energy creates matter, yet energy cannot be included in the classification of matter. This means, *matter is created out of no-matter, Something* out of *Nothing*.

Science cannot abandon its laws. It occupies itself only with such phenomena whose qualities can be proved empirically. But as *nothing* is not an object, and is not found in the sphere of phenomena which can be tested in laboratories, nor even through mathematical abstractions, science does not occupy itself with it.

But Kabbala does occupy itself with it. It is to Kabbala the essential of all essentials. Kabbala has a special name for Nothing. It calls it the Higher World, the world of Pure Will, the world of *Spirit*.

Kabbala compares Nothing (Ayin, Nihil) with such conceptions as *Wisdom*, as *Reason*. Since Wisdom is a *Something* which cannot be grasped by the senses, so *Nothing*, too, cannot be grasped by the senses. It is abstract, which can be grasped and comprehended only by the Soul. And the Soul comprehends it as the Spark of Divinity concealed within it. Nothing is the spirituality of the soul that comprehends it. And this Nothing, this spirituality reaches by various ways to the supreme attributes of Deity.

Kabbala explains it thus:

Everywhere is the Being of the Creator, Blessed be He, for everything has a quality, its individual taste, appearance, color, and the like. If we should separate this (abstract) quality from its matter, and consider it by itself, we will soon realize that there is not a thing which we can feel by touching it with our hands, or see with our eyes, but we comprehend it (abstract) through the soul in man. If so, it is surely a spiritual thing, and it is the expression of the Creator, Blessed be He, who rests in matter as a soul in the body.

This means:

When a man *sees*, let us say, a fruit, it gives him pleasure, because it is a definite material object. But when a man *thinks* of a fruit, *reminds* himself of it, imagines it, the fruit is a spiritual quality, has ceased to be real, and only the visionary image remains. But even this image can be considered as a conception of the physical senses. Yet when a man dismembers the image, and has in mind only one single quality of the fruit—its kind, appearance, size, quality, smell, taste, and he thinks of each detail separately, and concentrates on it, comprehends the essence of its being (what it is, the individual character), he is left with nothing actual, only an abstract, a quality that can be felt and understood only through the soul. That is the *Nothing* that is in everything—the Divine Spark within it.

There is a Divine Spark in every *thing* on earth; then how much more in the Crown of Creation of Man. More in one man and less in another, according to how the particular man comprehends the Divine. Nothing begins in man's consciousness where Reason ends, his reason which is based on his sense, and where his Divine intuition begins to reveal itself.

Wisdom is a positive thing—a Something. But what inspires and feeds Wisdom is Nothing. Nothing feeds the soul and fills it with light. Nothing is the inner sense of Creation, its streaming, flowing source. But its essence is hidden, and human understanding cannot comprehend it. The human mind is limited, has bounds. Nothing is boundless, has no limit. Nothing is the wonderful moment of Creation to which we can give no name. That is why we call it Nothing—non-existent, void.

Nothing is the spirit of the higher world, and expresses itself through the lower world. This is what the Zohar, the canonical book of Kabbala, says about it:

"All that is found and exists in the lower world has its spiritual counterpart in the higher world. There is not a thing in the lower world without its affinity in the higher world, dependent on it."

Kabbala uses the language of symbol. According to Kabbala, material things have no existence in themselves. They have a higher sense and significance. That is the way Kabbala interprets history.

Kabbala holds that the historic facts are not as important as the philosophy of history. That the empirical conception is unable to explain historical meaning—it lacks cosmic, transcendental and universal vision. Therefore it cannot possibly explain human problems.

For instance: if we interpret history as a chain of separate events, following each other in sequence, it will be only outside knowledge. It will not comprehend the process of development which brought these events about. History must be understood in its universal evolutionary process, not in the restricted limits of temporary events.

Take for example, the present process of the Return to Zion. It is not enough to connect it with such details as the Love of Zion Movement, the Bilu, Pinsker, Herzl, antisemitism, pogroms, the two World Wars and the extermination of a third of the Jewish People by the German Nazis. All these events are true, but the essential point goes much deeper and its history branches out more widely—it begins with the Patriarch Abraham, the first Monotheist, the Father of the Jewish People.

Of course, the actual facts cannot be excluded from any consideration of history. But the factual aspect must be considered only symbolically. The actual event has a meaning and significance over and beyond its immediate content.

The Zohar explains it in its own symbolic fashion:

"Thought is the essential and the beginning of all that exists, but it is not at first recognizable, and it is enclosed within itself. When thought begins to spread, it reaches the state of spirit, acquires the name Binah (understanding), and then it is no longer enclosed within itself. This spirit develops in the sheath of all the mysteries with which it is surrounded, and from it emerges the clear melody, which is the renewed harmony of all heavenly song."

Kabbala postulates that *Cause* is the secret of Existence. What the Cause is, is God's secret. From this premise it follows that man's individual sense is nothing but a reflection of the *universal* sense. Now as the human sense comprehends *Reason* in Existence, it is because Existence is a reasonable and understandable something. Every substance that is comprehended through our senses, every spiritual truth that stems from our consciousness, everything that is pictured in human imagination, proves the existence of a cosmic super-Reasoning sense, with which only the cosmic sense could have endowed man's sense and consciousness.

Thought seeks expression. It means that thought strives

to create a substance, an object which will symbolize it. This process of development which Kabbala calls the influence of absolute thought to become an object of its own, brings about its opposite, a Creation that in regard to thought is only relative. Why only relative? Because creation never reaches the level, the height of the Creator. But as the Creator cannot be recognized except through His expression, His creation, we get the idea of a lessening of the Creator, His diminution. This diminution of the Absolute is the cause of all troubles and pains. The Absolute, through His own quality, seeks to reabsorb the relative, the comparable. This absorption of the Absoluteness of the comparable is self-conscious. Therefore the self-destiny of God to attain *self*-consciousness is like the inner impulse of man to attain cosmic consciousness.

It means that in regard to the Absolute there is no higher stage than His *self*-consciousness. For man there is a higher stage—to know and to identify himself with the Absolute, that is, with the cosmic consciousness.

Since the effort to achieve self-consciousness is always accompanied by suffering, suffering becomes the means through which the Absolute attains His final aim. The same holds for man.

That is, after all, the process which in the language of philosophy is called dialectics, meaning the logic through which one object evolves out of another, which is its opposite. The German philosopher Hegel called it the dialectical method, through which the world-Reason works out the fundamentals of its development.

The fundamentals are that each substance, each idea transforms itself into its opposite—the thesis becomes anti-thesis, and the anti-thesis returns to its point of origin, to itself, enriched by its own contradiction. This creates the synthesis. The synthesis produces a new anti-thesis, which leads to a new synthesis, a new return to itself. And so the movement goes on, circle after circle, triad after triad—the synthesis of all that preceded it, and also a return to the first beginning.

This idea of the dialectical method, which Hegel arrived at only in the 19th century, was recognized by Kabbala hundreds of years before, and it expressed it in its own symbolic way, as follows:

"There is no light except it comes from darkness, for when the side of darkness becomes subordinated, then the Holy One, Blessed be He, rises up and is glorified. There is nothing created by His Holy Name except it comes from darkness. And there is no good except it comes from bad."

BUT WHAT is the nature of the Creation—this substance which is relative to its Creator, absolute thought?

Kabbala does not put this question so directly, and therefore it does not answer it so definitely. Yet the matter is one with which Kabbala does occupy itself, and as a result we derive—though not directly—both the question and the answer.

Existence is primarily an abstract concept. Physical existence is no more than the garment which the soul wears. Existence is the opposite of Non-Existence, Nothing, En, Nihil. But Nothing is not a void. It is in the final test Soul, Spirit, and that is *Eternal Existence*.

Nothing is essentially a *Thought*, the Thought of universal Reason, a moment of thinking. And thinking is a *something*, a *being*. Hence Nothing, Non-Existence, becomes again *Existence*. This is the way thought vibrates between its two opposites—*Existence* and *Non-Existence*, till it becomes its higher synthesis, *Becoming, Creating*.

In accordance with this thesis Kabbala explains the great mystery of Creation. The Zohar puts it this way: "All that exists, all that is created by His Holy Name, comes about through the union of (the two opposites) male and female.

In the Hegelian language of the dialectic method this may be interpreted as follows:

Male and Female are the thesis and anti-thesis, and their synthesis is Creation.

God Himself, Kabbala explains, is the synthesis of Male and Female. But to create the world He peeled off from His Absolute these necessary two attributes—Male and Female.

The attributes of God are: Yod, Hay, Vov, Hay. Yod and Vov are attributes of Male, while Hay is the Female attribute. In the beginning Yod paired with Hay, and later Vov with Hay. The pairing of Yod-Hay created the higher world, the world of spirit. The pairing of Vov-Hay created the lower world, the physical world. And these two worlds are also separate pairings—spirit is the Male, fertilizing the Female—the physical. In this way the world came into being, in its full perfection—Father and Mother, Son and Daughter.

THE ESSENTIAL thesis of Kabbala turns on the belief in the Unity of Creation, from which derives the unity and harmony of the universe. The Unity of the Godhead unites the transcendental, spiritual world with the immanent, physical world. According to Kabbala God is the Great Deep Sense, the Great Incomprehensible, the Mystery of Mysteries, Secret of Secrets. God is beyond human power of pictorial representation. The depth of Divine Wisdom is too high for human understanding to penetrate. God is the Original of Originality, the Secret of Secrecy, the Consciousness of Super-Consciousness.

Yet notwithstanding, this God expresses Himself in His full Power through the universe and through the love which is implanted in the human heart. The world is the reflection of God. There is a constant partnership interchange between the *Upper* and the *Lower*.

How does this interchange come about? Not directly between God and world. God is too illimitable direct to work on the world, which is limited. The interchange is effected through four of the Attributes of Divinity: Glory, Creation, Formation and Action. These Four Attributes, too, do not work directly on the world of worlds, the cosmos and all that is in it, but they employ for this the Ten Sephirot— Keter (Crown), Chochma (Wisdom), Binah (Understanding), Chesed (Grace), Geburah (Might), Tifferet (Beauty), Netzach (Triumph), Hod (Glory), Yesod (Foundation), Malchut (Kingdom).

The name Sephirot may be variously interpreted, and may be explained through different symbols. For instance, *Mispar*, which means Number, is evidence that their Number, Ten, is important as an indication of their definite effect in the Creation and Existence of the world, which was created by Ten Words; Sephira, sphere, is an indication that each separate Sephira has its own sphere of influence; also Sapir, the precious stone Sapphire, which shines with all the colors, is a sign that each separate Sephira is multi-colored and possesses within itself also part of the qualities of the other Sephirot, absorbs into itself the light of the other Sephirot, and they all influence each other.

Thus each Sephira develops three qualities—the quality it obtains from the other Sephirot, the specific quality for which it is fitted, the quality which it contributes to the other nine Sephirot.

There are lines of communication connecting the Sephirot with each other—nine through which each sends its influence to the other Sephirot, and nine through which each receives influences from the other Sephirot.

The Sephirot are influenced and influence. To what can this be likened? To every substance in the world. Each separate substance is on one side characteristically individually itself, and on the other side it draws influence and sustenance from the surrounding environment, which could even be its contrary. For instance, even the Crown of Creation, man, is a definite specific substance, a living creature. But he derives his sustenance from all sorts of sources: his physical sustenance from the sun, air, various foods; and his spiritual sustenance from the higher world, which is entirely outside his control, and is also not a living substance in the sense of life in the physical world, but is pure spirit, which has no form, and men cannot imagine it even in their widest imagination.

And all the Sephirot stretch through their complex lines of communication to Keter (Crown), the Crown of all Sephirot, through which their influence reaches to the En-Sof (the endless, the Infinite, the Attribute of the Godhead), and in their outcome all the Sephirot unite in the last Sephira, Malchut (Kingdom). Thus confirming again the great wonder of Echod (One). God is One, One is His Creation, One is the Law by which He rules and conducts the world.

The Creation is indeed One, but it comes into existence through the division and the mutual working of the sexes, Male and Female. Therefore the Sephirot too are divided into sexes, Male and Female, and it is according to their sexuality that their functions are determined—the Quality of Justice or the Quality of Mercy, Pure Reason or Emotion, Physical existence or Spirit—through the mingling of all the contraries we come to the source of *Existence*, the influence of the four letters of the Tetragrammaton, the Will of the Act of Creation, the ordering and the destiny of Existence.

THE ESSENTIAL book of Kabbala is the *Zohar*. The Zohar reveals to man through all kinds of explanations, symbols and allusions the Existence and the Unity of the Godhead, which fills the space of the universe and discloses itself to the human spirit in a glorious light of vast riches of color and radiance.

The Zohar is a collection of innumerable tales, fables,

parables, allegories, descriptions, flashes of thought, ideas, all set out in exalted poetic style. It tells of the greatness of the Heavens, through which it symbolizes spirit, and the deep abyss to which we can sink by denying spirit. It sings of the splendor of the stars and the richness of nature generally, and above all, man's relationship to the higher world.

The Zohar does not shut its eyes to the darker aspects of world and man. But that is the anti-thesis which could lead to the synthesis, the darkness through which we can emerge to the light, and the light is glorious beyond understanding. The Zohar discusses straight roads and crooked roads, Being and Not-Being, ways of life that proceed along straight roads, and such that are crooked, and it paints pictures that are clear and comprehensible, and others which are dim, unclear and strange—the joy of holiness against the pains and sufferings of the unclean. And all these contraries mingle there like happenings in a dream, like a fantastic dream within a dream, involved and tangled, yet cutting deep into mind and feeling.

The language and style of the Zohar is mystic. Everything is said by way of hints and allusions. It could not be otherwise. For how else reveal in our poor human language such exalted mysteries about God and Divinity, the essence of Being and Not-Being, of clean and unclean, pure and impure, physical and spiritual, that only a rich imagination can grasp? Therefore to understand the Zohar one must be competent to understand it, one must have a special inner sense which is able to recognize, as the Zohar does, how from darkness comes light and from bitter, sweet. Where an ordinary man sees shape and form one who steeps himself in the Zohar finds Divine song, wonderful melody, stretching from eternity to eternity.

All happenings, symbols and thoughts in the Zohar circle round one center—Rabbi Simeon ben Yohai and his collaborators. But they, too, are not clear, distinct figures, but are perceived as symbols, examples of the sublime, pure spirit in the garb of man.

Rabbi Simeon ben Yohai evolved the idea that the slightest stir of a man, even if only in intention, never becoming an act, reaches higher worlds, that one attains spiritual heights not only through specific dogmas, but essentially through the unique riches which are inherent in the *I* of a man, in his individual self, if only they are not squandered on things that profane the spirit of man. He also taught that all the senses enable us to see and hear all that can be touched and felt, that every object small and large, all there is in the world that has existence, is an approach to man, to recognize and appreciate the spiritual values as they deserve, and give them priority against the physical pleasures of the world.

For what is essential in man is his soul. The body is no more than a garment, a covering for the soul, the vessel which contains the spirit of man. The body departs. The spirit remains always. Not in the body but in the spirit is hidden man's destiny, from his first to his last moment, from the cradle to the grave.

There are in man three fields which find expression in each other—Body, Soul, and the Divine Spark. Through the limbs of his body and through his senses man recognizes his soul, and through the special senses of the soul he recognizes in himself the Divine Spark. But since he cannot, through the limitations of his physical senses, get a clear recognition of the soul, and he cannot through the limitations of the soul get a clear recognition of the Divine, man's knowledge is always unclear, on the borderline of knowing and not knowing.

Each day is a new revelation to man, a fresh Act of Creation. For nothing that was yesterday exists now, and nothing that exists now will be here later. Nothing repeats itself. Each moment brings something new, and each new thing is a separate spirituality, a separate experience. Days sweep past like shadows encircling a man. Each day in which nothing good was done returns to its Creator, God, shamed and humiliated. While on the other hand, if the day has been rich in good deeds, it weaves a spiritual garment for the soul which it will wear when it leaves the body.

All that man perceives round him is an indication of holiness. Therefore, whenever a man sees anything, he must have in mind the spiritual world, and the object towards which it points. For example, when one sees a rose with all its color, but the stalk has a thorn, one must know that this points to the *Shechina*, which is indeed the way of Mercy, but like the thorn on the stalk of the rose, is also the way of Judgment. Man must always derive reason from emotion and the sublime from the low.

The Zohar devotes much attention to a man's nature and occupation. It paints in bold colors the tangle of human thoughts, human desires, qualities and emotions, all leading to a recognition of the spirit of man. It discusses even human anatomy, the limbs, their forms and shapes, in which Kabbala sees an image that can lift the soul to high planes. Man who lives in lowness is able to lift himself to the heights.

The Kabbala develops in man the capacity and the desire to become conscious of the cosmos, to recognize the Divine. The Zohar, the essential book of the Kabbala, is a glorious Song of Songs, that is sung by the soul of man in its profound longing for union with its source, which is wrapped in the deep mystery of the Divine.

The great essential that the Kabbala strives to demonstrate is the importance of the human spirit. The Kabbala is full of indications of the great influence of the human soul—firstly, to attain its own bliss and, secondly, to bring redemption to all those worlds with which man is inevitably bound and connected. Man is man only because he has a soul, and the soul comes from the Divine Source. In this regard Kabbala differs from the Torah, which says, "Dust you are, and to dust you will return." And from Ecclesiastes who declares: "That which befalls the sons of men befalls the beasts." And from the Mishna (Ethics of the Fathers): "Know whence you came, from a putrefying drop. And where you are going, to a place of dust and worms." The Kabbala places man higher. It sees man as a spiritual being, coming from holiness and returning to holiness. There is a close relationship between the soul of man and the Divine Being. Man must not be considered a creature of flesh and blood and nothing more. His body is only his outer garb. The important thing is the soul; and that is holy.

According to Kabbala the soul is filled with longing for the Source—God. This is the idea continually repeated in the Zohar. The passages which speak of this great longing of the soul for the Divine Source are real poetry. In many places this love is compared to the love between man and woman; it is actually expressed in terms of sex. It is like the pairing of man and wife. But the use of this imagery must not be misinterpreted as erotic. It is, on the contrary, the pure lyricism of the Song of Songs. The Zohar speaks of sex as the cosmic union between the upper world and the lower. These two worlds are one, as in marriage, and the lower world which is symbolized as woman longs incessantly for its pairing with the upper world, to be fertilized by it.

THE KABBALA speaks in strictly symbolic language, so that it needs effort to understand it. I will try here to explain the matter as simply as I can.

People possess a great deal of knowledge about the world and its composition. How did they get this knowledge? Through experience and through searching. That raises a question—are human beings the only living creatures in the world with experience and the ability to search? All creatures have experience. Why can't they search? There are creatures whose species has lived on this earth longer than man. Why have they not crystallized out of their experience the knowledge that man has? The answer is: They haven't the capacity with which man has been endowed: Man has crystallized his experiences into knowledge because he possesses this ability.

Is this the truth? Or did man create this ability himself?

He didn't, says the Kabbala. Man was endowed with this ability before he had the understanding to give himself any account of its meaning.

Who endowed him with this ability? The answer to this is—Cause.

What Cause? The essence of Being.

What is Being? According to the Kabbala, Being is abstract, an idea, that is to say, which is comprehended by pure reason, and not through the physical senses.

Being is in essence the expression of the Divine through which it reveals itself to man. This is not the place for discussing whether God exists or not. What we are concerned with here is the attitude of the Kabbala. And the Kabbala is firmly convinced that there is a God, that He created the world and man, and He planted in man the ability to acquire knowledge through his human experiences. By giving man this ability God distinguished him from all other living creatures.

Therefore man is preordained from his creation to be different from all other creatures. By giving man this ability, God bestowed on him potentially the entire totality of knowledge that man has acquired till now and that he will acquire in the future, till the furthest reaches of time. It follows from this that God made man capable of all the knowledge that God Himself possesses.

As for the essential Kabbala, the Masters of Kabbala say it is no human creation, but the secret knowledge that God has revealed to man. Kabbala is endless, infinite as God is infinite. Therefore it could not have been created by anyone, only by God. God gave the Kabbala complete potentially to the first man, Adam.

But as Kabbala is a difficult matter, and it isn't every man who is capable of understanding it, it had to be transmitted generation by generation, not to all men, but to the few elect—from Adam to Moses, to the Elders, the Prophets, the Masters of the Kabbala, of whom Rabbi Simeon ben Yohai was the senior.

Now Adam is the symbol of mankind, for he is the father of *all* nations, not only the Jews. Hence we may say that God, through Adam, gave this knowledge to all *mankind*.

When God created Adam, meaning mankind, He endowed him with the capacity to obtain knowledge and understanding about God, the Creation, the ordering and the final destiny of Being, and the recognition of the quality and the predetermination of man. In other words, He gave to humankind the Kabbala in its full potential. It follows that it was not the Jews alone, but the all-human mind, that crystallized the Kabbala.

The Kabbala is the knowledge of all the mystic lore, the thought of all man's thoughts in his endeavor to penetrate to the secret of Existence. Indeed, Kabbala is Jewish, but it takes in all people who have developed a fruitful idea bearing on the mysteries of Being and Not Being.

At all times and everywhere, whenever and wherever the light of pure reason illuminated the human mind, people speculated about God, Life and Man. And their speculations produced theosophical systems. And these, as far as there is wisdom contained in them, are the prime source of Kabbala. There has not been a theological belief, however primitive and helpless it may have been, that did not make its contribution to the development of Kabbala. Man has always searched for God, even in his most primitive stages. It is the *searching* in which Kabbala is hidden, even if the searching is on false roads, and not towards the recognition of the developed idea of God.

Hence it follows that all theologies, no matter how primeval, all metaphysical philosophies, however primitive, all sciences, even if they are false, are all phases in the development of Kabbala, and have all given their meed towards establishing the way of the Kabbala.

The Kabbala is the evolutionary development of human thought—from the spiritual protoplasm till now, similar to man's physical evolution—from the biological protoplasm to his present state.

It may be useful here to draw an analogy between Einstein and the system developed in the Kabbala. Einstein, with the aid of mathematical formulas, explained his Expanding Field Theory, through which he expressed his belief that there is one sole cosmic law that rules the entire universe—time, space, matter, movement and energy. But even his genius could not go further than the physical world. Einstein did not reach the Lawgiver of this One Unified Law of the Universe. He could only make the concession that Spinoza had found the Lawgiver.

Now what Einstein's thought could not attain to, the Kabbala did. Like Einstein, Kabbala used a mathematical formula. But the mathematical formula Kabbala used took in all that Einstein proved, and also what Einstein had not reached—the Unity of the Law of the Universe and the Lawgiver. The formula used by Kabbala consists, as has already been said here, of four letters of the Hebrew alphabet—Yod-Hay Vov-Hay—which symbolizes the Lawgiver as one with His Law and takes in infinite Existence in its endless shapes and forms, including the act of creation, order and destiny, and the substance and fate of man.

We must understand, however, that the four letters of the Kabbala formula do not compose God's Name, as many think. They only constitute a formula through which we understand infinite Existence in its endless shapes and forms. According to Kabbala, God cannot be defined through a name, a formula, or anything else. Definition presupposes limitation and God is limitless. We must not even attempt to define God. Kabbala calls God by symbols, like Infinite, the Ancient Days and the like.

In astronomy, Kabbala is bound up with the Torah. But the Torah, says the Zohar, must be understood in two separate ways: the simpleness of the Torah, so that all can understand it, and the soul of the Torah, into which only the Masters of Kabbala can penetrate. The Zohar tells us the following:

"Rabbi Simeon ben Yohai said: Woe to the man who says the Torah came only to tell us simple stories and to show us ordinary things. For were it so we could today, too, compose a Torah of ordinary things, which would be even better than it (the Torah). If it is only to show simple things, there are writers today who could do this better. If so, let us proceed and compose a Torah of such a kind. But it is not so. The words of the Torah are sublime words, hints and allusions at unusual mysteries. Come and see: the higher world and the lower world are weighed in the same scale. Israel below and the angels above. When the angels come down to the lower world they wear the clothes of the lower world. For if they did not, they could have no existence here. And if that is true of the angels, how much more so of the Torah, through which the angels and the whole world were created, and everything exists only for its sake. When the Torah came down on *this* earth it had to dress in the clothes of *this* world—otherwise it could not endure it. The stories of the Torah are only its outer garb. Woe to him who takes the clothing for the true Torah. He will not have the life to come. Therefore, David said: 'Open my eyes, and I will see the wonders of Thy Torah, meaning what is hidden under the covering of the Torah. Come and see: There is a covering which all see. There are fools who see no more than the outer covering and look no further. But the body is more important than the covering, and the soul is more important than the body. It is the same with the Torah, which has a body, the commandments of the Torah, and this body is clothed in a garment—the history recorded there. Those who know better don't look at the garment, but at the body under the garment. And the wise men who serve the sublime King, who stand on the height of Mount Sinai, look deeper still, into the soul, which is the essential of everything, the essential of the Torah. In time they will be given the privilege to look even deeper, into the soul of the Torah."

The idea of Rabbi Simeon ben Yohai, that the essential of the Torah is its hidden symbol, and that the stories in it are appendages, is expressed more sharply in another place in the Zohar by Rabbi Eliezer who, dealing with the same subject, says:

"Come and see: A human king will not utter coarse speech, and he certainly will not write it down. So if the thought should come to you that God had no holy matters to write down out of which to create a Torah, and therefore He added all sorts of vulgar things like the words of Esau, of Hagar, what Laban said to Jacob, the speech of the ass, the words of Balaam, Balak, Zimri—that God collected all this together with the other stories and out of them composed a Torah—if such a thought should come to you; then you must ask—why does it call itself the Torah of Truth?"

Rabbi Eliezer comes to the same conclusion, that we must look under the garment of the Torah to seek the symbol, the soul of the Torah.

What is the soul of the Torah? That, the Kabbala teaches, is the deep significance which determines the Cause of all Causes, explains the Act of Creation, the order of existence, and the peculiar quality and destiny of man. All these mysteries are explained, expounded, interpreted through all sorts of hints and allusions which are concealed in every sentence, in each word, even in each letter of the Torah.

What is written in the Torah? Let us consider the Torah from the beginning. There is at the beginning of the Torah a rational account of how the world was created, how man came to be, how man spread over the earth, how the Jewish People came into existence, and so on but these stories, are according to Kabbala, only the outer garb of the Torah. Afterwards come the commandments, the customs and the judgments of the Torah. All that we can learn, and it is easy to understand, because it is presented in simple language. But, say the Kabbalists, we must not take the Torah simply, as it is transmitted in its usual understandable language. We must penetrate to the essential of the Torah, to its soul; And the soul does not speak in ordinary language. Each letter—even the appearance of each separate letter, each word, each sentence of the Torah, has a different meaning, is an allusion at something, a deep hidden thought.

For example: The Torah begins with the word Bereshit. Bereshit means In the Beginning. The word in Hebrew consists of six letters. On the surface it is not strange that the Torah begins with this word, and the first letter in this first word is Bet (B), which is not the first, but the second letter of the Hebrew alphabet. It seems natural that the Torah should begin with a word that means "In the Beginning." That word is Bereshit.

But Kabbala sees it differently. First of all, Kabbala considers it according to mathematical symbols, and interprets it with a definite formula. Each letter represents a number. Bet is 2, Resh is 200, Aleph is 1, Shin is 300, Yod 10, Tov 400. Then there is a meaning given to the specific appearance of each letter and the order of the letters, their sequence in the Hebrew alphabet.

Then there is the question, why does the Torah begin with the second letter of the alphabet, not the first. If it is the Beginning, the Beginning of the world, it should begin logically with the beginning of the alphabet.

This is the way it is answered: The first letter of Bereshit is Bet. Bet is 2. From this the Kabbala derives the belief that 2,000 years before God created the world He wrote the Torah. The Torah was the plan according to which God created the world. God created the Torah in Hebrew. God had the letters of the Hebrew alphabet in His mind from eternity.

When God thought of writing the Torah all the letters of the Hebrew alphabet appeared before Him, and each separate letter pleaded that it should be the one to begin the Torah. Each had its own claim to be chosen for the honor. God listened to them all, and decided to begin the Torah with Bet, because Bet begins the word Brachah (Blessing), which is the symbol of happiness.

God said to the letters: All of you can be understood only through that letter. I shall create the world to bring its existence happiness.

This is symbolic. Let us consider the symbol indicated here by Kabbala.

When we consider actions and strivings we realize that all our conscious activities and ambitions have a definite aim. But all the aims we set ourselves in life derive from one source—the desire for happiness. Happiness is the goal towards which every rational human activity strives. This holds true for other creatures. They, too, seek happiness, even though they lack the sense of consciousness. They seek it through their instincts.

This universal aim of Existence—Brachah, blessing, happiness—which begins with the Bet of Bereshit, Beginning, is the Cause of all Causes, of the Intention God had to create the world.

Each separate letter of the Hebrew alphabet symbolizes a

virtue—Freedom, Justice, Righteousness, Mercy, Love. And each letter advanced its own claims why Torah should begin with it. But God said: All your virtues can exist only in happiness. Your virtues are the means through which happiness can be attained. Without happiness, by themselves, your virtues have no value.

Therefore God began the Torah with Bet, the formula for Brachah, for blessing, for happiness.

Kabbala proceeds: The fact that Bet also denotes the numeral 2 symbolizes the duality of the world. In philosophy it is expressed through the idea thesis and anti-thesis; in physics through the positive and negative parts of matter containing energy. Kabbala sees these two relationships as the phenomenal (physical) and transcendental (spiritual) relationships of Existence, including such relationships as masculinity and femininity, fatherhood and motherhood, reason and intuition.

Kabbala views it with its own logic: Take the letter Bet away from the word Bereshit, and what remains? Reshit—Beginning. What was Beginning? Beginning was supreme wisdom before He divided Himself into Yod-Hay and Vov-Hay masculinity and femininity—in order to create the world in its contrary theses which synthesize in Glory. And this: The word Bereshit contains the two letters Shin and Tov. Their union produces the word Shet, Six. Hence Kabbala infers that God created the world through six of the Ten Sephirot; that God created the world in six days; that he gave the world six directions—East, West, South, North, Above and Below. And the last letter of Bereshit—Tov—is also the last letter of Emet, Truth. It means that Truth is the final aim of the Act of Creation.

WHAT I HAVE set out here is but a feeble indication of how Kabbala regards the Torah. I have considered only one word, Bereshit. The Kabbala deals in the same way with the whole Torah.

The essential idea from which Kabbala derives its ecstasy and devotion is its profound faith in the Unity of God and His Creation and the spiritual relationship of man to the Divine.

What is God? Spinoza said God is His own Cause. Other philosophies say that God is the Prime Cause. The Kabbala in its view takes in these ideas, also regards God as the Cause of all Causes and the Foundation of all Foundations—both of Himself and of all Causes—from the First to the Last—One!

THE INFINITE, MAN
AND MESSIAH

THE MESSIANIC IDEA

THE TRAGEDY of the Jewish expulsion from Spain in 1492 cast depression and despair over the minds of Jews wherever the news of the disaster reached. The Spanish expulsion and the Inquisition, accompanied by persecution and massacres in other cities of Europe where Jews were living, plunged the Jews into complete consternation.

But the Jews are always full of hope. Without hope Jews could never have survived their long history of martyrdom. They would long ago have perished, both as a group and as individuals. Though their sufferings were cruel, they were sure they would not last forever. Messiah, the Redeemer, would come—must come! The Prophets had foretold his coming. He tarried, but he would come! And with him would come the new dawn, such bright light that it would compensate for the present darkness.

So then too after the Spanish expulsion, when Jewish sufferings were intense, the ancient Jewish yearning for the Messiah also became more intense. The Messianic idea was firmly planted in Jewish belief for centuries, from the time of the Prophets. The Messianic idea was one of the cardinal principles of the Jewish faith. And this gave the Jewish people courage and strength to endure the sufferings it had encountered on its long road in history.

When the Jews still lived in their own land, whenever affliction fell upon them, and afterwards in exile, when their sufferings increased, dreamers and warriors arose among them, with a vast power of vision, steeped in mysticism and full of faith in miracles, and they were proclaimed, or they proclaimed themselves, Messiahs, or the people considered them such against their own wish and will. There were some imposters and adventurers among them, but most of them were convinced that they had been called to fulfill a holy mission. They are known as false Messiahs only because the evil they undertook to sweep away was too powerful for their limited strength, and it destroyed them. If Bar Kochba had prevailed against the Romans, he would have remained Bar Kochba, Son of the Star. But he failed, so he was called Bar Koziba, Son of Lies.

The people were always bitterly disappointed in the Messiahs who arose from time to time, but their faith in the Messiah never lessened. The worse things became, the stronger was their hope that the Messiah would come and bring redemption. This belief reached its culmination after the Spanish expulsion.

Terrible was the fate of those who were expelled from Spain. Of three hundred thousand who went into exile, only a tenth were able to save themselves. The rest died of hunger and cold, perished on the sea or in the deserts, were captured by pirates, who slew many and sold the rest as slaves. There was only one consolation; they believed that:

These are the sufferings that are the prelude to Redemption, the deep darkness that comes before the dawn. These are the birth-pangs of the Great Bright Day of Salvation. Soon the Anointed Saviour, Messiah ben David, will come and will redeem the people of Israel, the shining star for all mankind.

But to make it possible for Messiah to come, man must be good and devout; he must always have God's sanctity within him, and rise to the heights. But these heights are hard to reach in exile.

When the Jews were in their own land and they sinned, they brought about the destruction of the Temple and their own exile. But they still had one great consolation—and this they all believed—that God had not forsaken them. God had withdrawn Himself from them, but He had left them His Shechina, Metatron, who watched over God's children, the Children of Israel. Metatron had detached himself from God and had gone with the Jews into exile. He accompanied them everywhere, from exile to exile, from land to land. He suffered all their pains and shared all their torments. But it would not always be like that. The great End of Days would finally come, the Redemption, the Messianic era.

BUT LONG before the Spanish expulsion, we had glorious descriptions of how Messiah would appear among us. One such description is in the Midrash, in Sefer Zerubabel, by an unknown author, believed to have lived in Italy in the 9th or 10th century. The Midrash is written in the style of the Book of Daniel.

Zerubabel, who, the Midrash tells us, was a descendant of King David, wanted to discover when Messiah would come. Then a wind (or Spirit—Ruach) lifted him up and brought him to "the City of Blood" (Rome). There he went to the market place, and there he met a man, ugly and repulsive, who told Zerubabel that he was Messiah. Zerubabel looked at the creature with abhorrence and fear and disbelief. Then suddenly there was a miracle. The man was transformed. Ugly as he had been, he now was radiant with light, and his face shone gloriously. Zerubabel knew at once that this was truly the Redeemer! For this is God's Will, that the Saviour who will redeem the People of Israel, and with them the whole world, must sit fastened with chains, and suffering great pain, in this "City of Blood," Rome, till the End of Days will come, and God will remember to save His People, Israel.

As Zerubabel stood there astonished and wondering, there appeared to him the Angel Metatron, God's Messenger, and revealed to him the great Mystery:

Messiah was born immediately after the Destruction of the Second Temple. God had sent a great wind (Spirit), and it had lifted up Messiah and carried him to Rome, and set him down there till the Glorious Day of the Redemption comes. And the Angel Metatron also revealed to Zerubabel the mystery of what will happen after the End of Days:

The name of the Redeemer who revealed himself to you, he said, is Menachem ben Emiel. Before the time comes for him to reveal himself, his forerunner will appear, Messiah ben Joseph, whose name is Nehemiah ben Hoshiel. Ben Joseph will gather exiles together and will bring them to Jerusalem, where the People will serve God with great devotion for three full months.

Then Metatron showed Zerubabel the stone figure of a woman, and said: Know that Satan will lie with this, and of that union will be born the great wicked one, Armilus. This son of the Evil One and this stone figure will be terrible in appearance—hairy all over with red hair. He will be twelve cubits in height, and his arms will reach down to his ankles. No one will be able to withstand Armilus. He will conquer the whole world. He will slay Messiah ben Joseph, and will again disperse and scatter the Sons of Israel over the whole earth. When Messiah ben Joseph is slain, his staff will, by God's command, pass into the hands of Hephzibah, the mother of Messiah ben David. This is the same miraculous staff with which Moses divided the Red Sea. The staff afterwards came to King David. It had belonged to Adam and Seth. Elijah ben Eliezer kept the staff in a cave near Tiberias. Messiah ben Joseph fetched it out of there. With this staff in her hands, Hephzibah the mother of Messiah ben David, will come forward, and all the stars in heaven and the constellations, will war for her, and she will defeat two powerful Kings, the worst enemies of Zion.

This will come to pass when 990 years will be completed from the time of the Destruction of the Temple (in the year 1058). Then Hephzibah will give the miraculous staff to her son, Menachem, Messiah ben David, and he, the illustrious Saviour, will appear in the Valley Arbol.

At the call of the Messiah and Elijah the Prophet, Messiah ben Joseph, will rise from the grave. And these three, together, the illustrious Saviour, Elijah and ben Joseph, will enter Jerusalem. All the martyrs who perished for His Name's Sake will rise from their graves. The earth will tremble to its foundations, and the redeemed Children of Israel will assemble jubilantly from all the corners of the earth. Then Messiah will, with the breath of his mouth, slay the wicked Armilus, the Temple will be rebuilt, and the People of Israel will inherit the land for ever.

The coming of the Messiah is pictured even more vividly in the Zohar:

Before Messiah appears, a great shining star will rise in heaven, like the bright day. And a great flame will ascend in heaven from the North. The star and the flame will stand forty days in heaven, and all the people on earth will tremble and shake with fear. At the end of the forty days a war will break out between the star and the flame, for the flame will want to swallow up the star. In the end the victory will be with the star, and flame will be quenched. After that, the star, too, will be quenched, and even at noon it will be so dark that it will not be possible to see either heaven or earth—dark as the world was when the Temple was destroyed. And a voice will be heard, descending from heaven with thunder and lightning, and the earth will tremble, and a great confusion will come upon the world. Then Messiah will appear in the Garden of Eden, and all the saints will crown him. And a voice will call out powerfully from the branches of the trees in the Garden of Eden:

"Rise, you holy ones of God, rise for the Messiah!" And all the holy martyrs and saints will gather round Messiah. Abraham will stand at his right hand, Isaac at his left, Jacob in front of him, and Moses will lead the dance. From the Garden of Eden, Messiah will be taken to God, and God will kiss him, and over the Infinite, the En-Sof, 390 heavens will form. And God will turn to one heaven that was prepared for this from the six days of Creation, and out of a space in this heaven, He will take out a crown, and will, with it, crown Messiah. Then God will kiss him again, and all the angels in heaven will bring him gifts.

A pillar of light will descend upon the earth, so bright, that nothing like it has been seen in the world before. With this light shining on him, Messiah will come to Rachel's Tomb; he will comfort Mother Rachel, and will tell her the great news of the Redemption. On that day the whole world will tremble; and all people who had occupied themselves with the Torah will come to Messiah, and young children, innocent of sin, will gather round him, and will give him the strength to perform great miracles. At the same time, all the Jews who are scattered and dispersed over all the corners of the earth will collect round Messiah. And the Shechina, too, which till now was in exile, will be redeemed from exile, together with the Jews, and it will be joined back again with its Lord, with God.

DON ISAAC ABRAVANEL

AFTER THE expulsion of the Jews from Spain, Don Isaac Abravanel was the man who was at the head of the wandering exiles, and he was, also the man who brought them the glowing promise of the Redemption.

Abravanel was by temperament a rationalist, not a mystic. He was an economist and financier. He had, by his services in this field, won the trust and favor of the Spanish King Ferdinand, who had, with his wife, Queen Isabella, signed the decree expelling the Jews, for which he had received the blessing of the Grand Inquisitor Torquemada. Abravanel could have stayed on in Spain after the expulsion, but he chose to go into exile with rest of his people. He was fated to wander from land to land, till he found a refuge first in Monopoli, in Southern Italy, and then in Venice.

When he died, Abravanel left a rich legacy of his literary works. He was not so much an original thinker as a man who was philosophically trained and disciplined, with a profound faith in the fundamentals of Judaism. The tragedy of the Jewish expulsion from Spain made Abravanel direct his thoughts wholly to the hope of the coming of the End of Days and the Redemption. In that regard he gave expression to the feelings of all Jews, who had never ceased to pray for the coming of the Messiah.

Abravanel tells us, in the foreword of his book MA-YENE HA-YESHUAH ("The Sources of Salvation") how he came to the Messianic idea. He pictures in terrifying colors, the sufferings to which the fleeing Jewish exiles from Spain found themselves exposed in their wanderings. "Worn out, dispirited, bent down to the ground, the hapless wanderers cried, 'We have no strength left! We have no more hope!' It was then I decided in my heart—No more waiting! We must help the falling, support the weak, lift up those who despair!'"

Abravanel goes on to tell how he kept tirelessly searching in the holy writings to discover "When will be the End of Days, the Messianic Age? When will the glorious Redeemer come?" He wanted to find the answer, to proclaim the good tidings to the poor refugees, to tell them that the day of Salvation was near.

But the answer was not easy to find. The words of the Prophets are deep and profound and obscure—it is hard to penetrate the veil that conceals the secret of future times. The Midrash Zerubabel says that Messiah will come in the year 990 after the Destruction of the Temple. Many years have passed since that date, and Messiah has still not come. So there must be a mistake in the calculation. But Messiah *will* come. He *must* come. And he, Abravanel, must discover the true date.

Abravanel did not cease to seek the answer. And at last he found it in the Book of Daniel. In his MA-YENE HA-YESHUAH he relates how and what he found in the Book of Daniel. He analyzes every verse, each dark saying in the Book of Daniel. He calls Daniel a saint, a God-fearing man, and a true Prophet through whom the Holy Spirit spoke. To Abravanel, Daniel had in his visions, discovered everything that would come to pass at the End of Days. And he had written it all down in his Book in the form of hints and allusions. Daniel foresaw all the troubles and sorrows that would afflict the Jewish People, and also the bright glorious luminous End, when God's Messenger, Messiah ben David, will come and redeem the Jewish People from exile and dispersion.

Abravanel tells us that after great effort he succeeded in finally unravelling the mystery and revealing through hints and allusions, and through Gematriah, the hidden secret in the Book of Daniel, that the Messianic pangs would begin in the year 1503, and that the great Redemption would come not later then 1535.

Abravanel foretold the Redemption, and the people hearkend to him, and prepared to receive the Redeemer.

For Messiah can come only when the people will be fit and prepared to receive him. And this preparation is not possible in any other way than through living a good life, doing good. That can hasten the End, and Messiah will speed his coming. But otherwise, it will only prevent his coming, and Messiah will not appear till the previously described time—a time that may still be very distant.

So people began at that time of affliction and trouble, to make great preparations for receiving Messiah. People immersed themselves in Kabbala, studied the Zohar, searched it for indications and inferences to show when Messiah would come, to show that his coming was very near.

DAVED REUBENI AND SHLOMO MOLKO

Two PLACES in the Turkey of those days, Salonica and Adrianople, became the cities of refuge for the exiles. Thousands of Jewish refugees from Spain settled there, including a number of scholars, sages, and Kabbalists. And these two cities became the great centers of Jewish spiritual life in the Diaspora. A little later came a third city, Safad, in the Land of Israel, where dedicated Jewish men and Kabbalists went to dwell. From Safad the great mystical movement and the preparations for the coming of the Messiah spread to all the corners of the Jewish Dispersion.

At that time, two Jews appeared, who at first brought great hopes into the Jewish world; but these hopes ended afterwards in bitter disillusionment. They were David Reubeni and Shlomo Molko.

David Reubeni appeared on the scene like the sudden rise of a marvellous legend. He claimed to be a brother of Joseph, who was, he said, the King of a powerful Jewish Kingdom in South Arabia—the Jews who lived there, he declared, were descended from the Ten Tribes. To this day we have not cleared up the mystery who David Reubeni really was. He has remained a riddle. Was he an adventurer and a swindler, as some historians describe him? Or was he a Jew who felt the Jewish misery intensely, and wanted to bring the Jewish redemption in his own way? He negotiated with diplomats, with Princes and Kings and with the Pope. He created a stir, a great sensation in the world.

He made a dramatic entrance into Rome in 1524, riding on a white horse, and attended by a large retinue. He said he had come as the representative of his brother, King Joseph, to discuss with the Pope and the Kings of Christian Europe, the supply of guns and cannon for his Jewish Kingdom in Arabia, to wage war against the Turkish Sultan, to expel him from the region of the Red Sea, and to liberate the Land of Israel from Moslem rule.

He was received by Pope Clement VII, and seems to have impressed the Pope. He then went to Portugal, where King John III received him royally.

Jews all over the world began to expect great happenings. He raised tremendous hopes among the secret Jews in Portugal and Spain—the Marranos—who had outwardly become Catholics, but under that cover continued to practice Judaism. The very idea of a Jewish Kingdom somewhere, and the story of the Ten Lost Tribes still living an independent life in their own sovereign State seemed to Jews like the prelude to the coming of the Messiah.

One young Marrano in Portugal, Diego Pires, was so excited by it that he avowed himself a Jew, and took the Jewish name Shlomo Molko. He was a young man of 25 when Reubeni came to Portugal, and being born a Christian, had access to the Royal Court. He held an important position in the High Court. He was a greatly talented young man, with soldierly qualities, yet also gifted with a mystical, poetic nature, a visionary and a believer in dreams. David Reubeni's coming seemed to him the fulfillment of his dreams.

He went to Reubeni, and said to him: "I am now a Jew, like all Jews. Will you reveal your secrets to me?'"

But Reubeni was afraid that it might be said that he had influenced Shlomo Molko to abandon Christianity and become a Jew. So he urged Molko to leave Portugal quickly, before the Inquisition got to know about his defection. Molko listened to him, and went to Turkey, first to Adrianople, and then to Salonica, where he became acquainted with the famous Kabbalist, Joseph Taytazak, who taught him Kabbala. He immersed himself in Kabbalistic studies and began to experience strange states of exaltation. He had visions, and thought himself able to prophesy and foretell the future. He wandered from town to town, from land to land, preaching passionately about the Messianic mission of David Reubeni, whom he saw as the forerunner of the Messiah.

Shlomo Molko's fine, handsome appearance, his great knowledge of Kabbala, his eloquence, his profound faith, won him the enthusiastic support, not only of ordinary people, of the common folk, but of distinguished scholars, who became his ardent champions. He convinced many of his hearers that the End had already arrived, that the powerful Turkish Empire would soon crumble and collapse, and the Holy Land would be open for Jewish refugees. People believed him. They believed when he told them, that he, Shlomo Molko, had been sent to bring the great tidings that the Day of Judgment for the world was at hand.

Shlomo Molko announced that he was going to the capital of the world, chastising Rome, where God's chastening sword would be lifted, and the Great Day of Judgment would begin.

And to Rome Shlomo Molko went. From there he addressed an open letter to his friends telling them how he had been received with enthusiasm. At first he was regarded with Hostility, suspected of some association with Christendom's arch-enemy, the Turkish Sultan. He was for a time in mortal danger.

When he saw the gates of Rome, he wrote in his letter, the city which was the symbol of the Destruction of Jerusalem and of the humiliation of the Jewish People, the floodgates of tears in him were opened, and he wept and prayed to the Creator and Ruler of the world that He should change His wrath to favor. Then he heard a voice call to him from on high: "Seir (Christendom) will fall into the hands of its enemy. The People of Israel will show their power. God will take mercy upon His servants. He will exact vengeance, and He will pay what is due."

In the twelfth month, Adar 1530, his letter continued, a deep sleep had fallen upon him at midnight, and he had seen the old man who had previously revealed himself to him. And the old man said to him: "My son, I have come to reveal to you what will happen to the nations among who myou dwell. Come to the ruins of Jerusalem with me, the ruins that you have visited once before!"

The old man had brought him to the Land of Israel, and there he had seen various creatures in the shape of marvellous birds of all colors, and signs of fire had appeared in heaven. And the old man had said to him: "Know, my son, the great bird you saw is the warning of a flood and an earthquake. The flood will be in a land in the north, and the earthquake in the land of your birth (Portugal). Afterwards there will be great miracles, and the great and only Day will come, the True Divine Day, the Day of Wonder."

Shlomo Molko met a tragic end. He came to Regensburg for an audience with the Emperor Charles V, who turned him over to the Inquisition, and he was burned at the stake.

SHLOMO MOLKO'S death as a martyr only added to his holiness in the eyes of the people. His Messianic movement did not end with his death. And when the time came and passed when according to the calculations of Abravanel and afterwards of Shlomo Molko, the Messiah should have appeared and he did not appear, there were Kabbalists who soon produced other calculations that the Messiah would come later. And the people believed and waited and did not cease to hope.

Before long there was a change in the Messianic movement. People began to realize that the Land of Israel and not the Diaspora, was the proper place to receive the Messiah—

Eretz Israel, the land where the Shechina always dwells, and where, as Yehuda Halevi said, "The air is full of souls." The Zohar also contributed to this result, through its affirmation that "Happy is the man who is privileged to dwell in Eretz Israel, and can find union with the sacred soil. He has the privilege of the dew of heaven which descends upon the earth, and he will after death be privileged to find union with the Holy earth in Heaven. He will have the privilege of the Holy Spirit resting upon him always."

Eretz Israel became the center of the great Messianic movement. And Safad was the town where the Kabbalists came to dwell and where they established their Yeshivas. One of the main reasons why Safad was chosen was its proximity to Meron, which was the tomb of Rabbi Simeon ben Yohai, who according to Kabbalist belief was the author of the Zohar.

There were three great men at that time who stood out on Kabbalist thought, and erected the vast edifice of Jewish mysticism, which raised human personality to the pitch of ecstasy, and evolved a deep faith in the ultimate triumph of what is good and just.

The first of these three giants was Meir ben Ezekiel Ibn Gabbai, who did not himself gain the privilege of dwelling in the Holy Land. The other two were Moses Cordovero and Isaac Ashkenazi Luria (the Holy Ari) who both settled in Safad. Their influence spread into every corner of the world where Jews dwelled.

MEIR BEN EZEKIEL IBN GABBAI

MEIR BEN EZEKIEL Ibn Gabbai was born in Spain in the 15th century. He was only eleven when the expulsion from Spain made him a wanderer. He found refuge in Turkey, but we don't know in which town, though it was probably Adrianople or Salonica, where most of the exiles found refuge.

He wrote a number of books on Kabbala, where he considered the problem which always occupied the minds of the Kabbalists—how, out of the Absolute Echod, the One, which is all spirit and is above and beyond all possibility of change, could there develop anything so small and petty as this temporary, transient, ever-changing matter? He went very deeply into this question in one of his books, DERECH EMUNAH ("The Way of Faith").

"Divinity," says Ibn Gabbai, "which is the Prime Cause of all Causes, is altogether higher than human understanding. It cannot be conceived nor cognized nor imagined. It cannot even be designated by a Name, for names distinguish one thing from another, but there is no other from which to distinguish God. All the designations through which God is known and called upon are no more than human linguistic terms that man uses to convey his idea of matters that are hidden and higher than his understanding. God's Name is therefore One with the divinity, co-eternal and incomprehensible, like the Prime Cause itself, which, too, is beyond comprehension.

"And the unmentioned and incomprehensible, ineffable Name," Ibn Gabbai proceeds, "contains in itself all Ten Sephirot, which are not born and not created, but are emanations from God—since they, the Sephirot, are the various manifestations revealing God's Being. God's Being does not alter or change. He creates nothing new—He only emanates, radiates—and the Divinely concealed forces are revealed through the Sephirot and are brought from the potential to reality. The Sephirot are the intermediaries, the links between the Cause and the Creature. They are the tools with which the world came to be and exists.

"As God's emanations, the Sephirot are one Being with God, and therefore they are like God co-eternal and infinite. Only in that they are emanations and receive God's abundance—in that alone lies a departure and a lessening, a diminution. And this makes it possible for them to create the finite and transient."

The Sephirot, Ibn Gabbai continues his line of thought, are the multifarious revelation of the Divinity, and only through their multifariousness is man able to receive them. It is to them, to the Sephirot, to the emanations of God and not to God Himself, that man's prayers rise, for it is they alone whom flesh and blood can comprehend, it is they alone whom man addresses with all his praises, and crowns with all the attributes of Divinity.

Yet the Sephirot must not be conceived as separate and independent, for the emanations are within Divinity, and not outside it; and as the human soul reveals itself through the limbs of the body, so Divinity, the soul of all the emanations, reveals itself through the Sephirot. And in the same way as a man's soul is only one, notwithstanding all the different actions and achievements of his limbs, so too, are the Sephirot, God's attributes, an absolute unity, one with God. For the multifariousness, all the differences are not in the Divine and in the Divine attributes, but are in us and in our ideas. God is One!

Man, with his limited conceptions, is not otherwise able to receive the revelation of God's doings. Therefore, he sees them in many ways and in many colors. But God is only One and changeless. There are in Him no differences and no contradictions, so that God would be now the God of mercy and now the God of justice. He appears to us like that only because we, with our limited comprehension, cannot receive, cannot comprehend the Nature of God in any other way. When we speak of God's wrath or of God's grace, we do not express in that way God's true Nature. We only say how *we* understand and assess God's doings. The same sun-ray, Ibn Gabbai points out, brings different and often contradictory results: it bleaches linen and bronzes a man's skin; it softens pitch and hardens wax. If it passes through a prism the same ray shines with many colors. Yet we know it is only one, not many.

This, he says, is the deeper meaning of our sages' observation, that before the Creation, God was One, and His Name One Alone—that before the world was created, His multifariousness could not be revealed, since there were no creatures yet, each to perceive God's whole Unity and Changelessness, according to his understanding, in limited and changeable forms.

But what is the purpose that brought about the Act of Creation? Ibn Gabbai asks. What was the intention in the creation of the world and of its crown, man?

His answer is that thought obtains its supreme consummation when it becomes embodied in achievement, in the act of will, and passes from the potential to action, to performance, to realization. The supreme consummation of God's Will, of God's Thought, the supreme test, their revelation, can be achieved only through action, through deed, by becoming concrete through the action, through fulfillment. This is why the world of reality was needed. For the deed, the revelation of the Act of Will, through which, alone, abstract thought attains its supreme consummation, cannot happen outside space, outside the real world. Our world, therefore, is a necessary link for the higher worlds to attain their consummation, and it creates the possibility of God's Will revealing itself in all its full splendor.

In the center of Creation stands God's pride and crown—man, whose spark is a reflection of God's Will and whose soul is a spark from the rays of all the Sephirot.

Then Ibn Gabbai enters into a sharp dispute with Maimonides, who was influenced by Greek philosophy. Here, says Ibn Gabbai, we can see clearly the contradiction between the world conception of Greek philosophy and the Jewish point of view. According to Aristotle, God is the Absolute Infinite Thinking Prime Source, whose effect on the order of the world does not consist in the world being ruled by God's creative and effective Will-Power. God influences the world not through what He does and achieves, but only by the fact that He *is* and *thinks* and is completely filled with the consciousness of his Nature. Aristotle's God is not the ruler of the world. He is only *Thought*, Eternal and eEdless *Thought*. But the Jewish God, says Ibn Gabbai, is not the remote God who stands outside the world, but is the God who creates, who embraces the whole world and sustains the whole world.

It is impossible, by cold reason, by dry analytical thought, to comprehend the Jewish God, to rise to the course of life and of existence. The Jewish God is the God of Revelation, of the Great Miracle, and only through profound intuition, through religious pathos and religious ecstasy, can we glimpse His Light.

Not philosophic speculations and theoretical logical assumptions are important, but ethical perfection, the desire to embody in life the ideal of righteousness, to reveal through actions, the will to approach closer to the Holy and Divine.

To Ibn Gabbai, the purpose of the world was clear and comprehensible. He had no doubt that the soul of man was very high, belonged to a very high level, that the Zaddik is the supporting pillar of the world, and that all creatures are subject to his will. On what is the Zaddik's immense power based? On the Torah with all its commandments, says Ibn Gabbai. The Torah is the emanation, the radiation of the Divine Wisdom, the embodiment of God's Name; it is the pathfinder, the sure guide how to incorporate the Divine Will in concrete actions. Thanks only to the Torah and its commandments, man takes part, participates in the union of the Divine with its supreme perfection and incomparable glory. Not knowledge alone is important—knowledge not accompanied by good deeds, is like a lifeless mass, a Golem. Every good deed performed by a man has its echo reverberating in the higher spheres, and it leads man to the highest stages, brings him near to God.

But man, says Ibn Gabbai, is not presented with immortality merely as a reward for being good. It isn't the reward that matters. There is a much higher aim, the ultimate end and purpose, which is to praise God's Name and to reveal His Glory. This supreme purpose needs no other reward. Its one and only motive power must be limitless, absolutely dedicated and devoted love. And this limitless love of God must be accompanied with complete devoted love of one's human equal, one's fellow man, each individual man separately, who is a spark of the Divine. Man should not be content with the commandment to love your neighbor as yourself—his love should be so intense and so powerful that he would love his neighbor more than himself.

Ibn Gabbai is scornful of "alien" sciences. The true knowledge of nature and the world and its creatures lies not in Aristotle's physics—as interpreted by Maimonides—but in the Act of Creation revealed in the Divine Torah. He puts all the emphasis on how important it is for the People of Israel to observe the commandments of the Torah. The People of Israel who concluded the eternal covenant with God's Torah, is the guardian and protector of the world. Jewish thought and reasoning are lighted up, illuminated by the foundations of the Torah. Therefore, Jews must not depart from the right road. If they do, they falsify the Holy Covenant that they have concluded with the Torah; if they do not fulfill its commandments they lose their wonderful power and are given over to be slaves to slaves. If a Jewish soul has sinned and has not fulfilled its great mission, it is incapable of returning to its sources till it has washed itself clean from its sins.

That souls is condemned to wander over the earth, reincarnated not only into other people, but even into animals, till it has been completely purified, and attains the highest stage of perfection. When all souls will have been purified through the process of reincarnation, the great Redeemer, Messiah ben David, will appear.

THESE ARE the essential points of Ibn Gabbai's system in Kabbala, and it was on these essential points that the two most profound and most influential Kabbalists in Safad, Moses Cordovero and Isaac Ashkenazi Luria, who left their stamp on the further development of Jewish mystical thought, built their systems. Moses Cordovero was the most profound thinker of the Sephardic theoretical Kabbala system, and Isaac Ashkenazi Luria was the no less profound thinker of the system of the Ashkenazic practical Kabbala. Cordovero developed all the abstract ideas about God and His world and His creatures, about spirit and matter—the ideas with which the Sephardic abstract Kabbala was engrossed, and Isaac Luria developed all those ideas which are concerned with man and his actions, fasting and self-mortification to suppress the material needs—all the ideas with which the Ashkenazic practical Kabbala is full.

RABBI MOSES CORDOVERO

WHAT CONSTITUTED Rabbi Moses Cordovero's Kabbala? Like many others before him, including Ibn Gabbai, and like many after him, Rabbi Moses Cordovero was confronted by the same old question—How did it come about that a purely spirit All-Good, Absolute, One and Changeless God should have created a world which is material, full of faults, containing so much evil, so many differences contradicting each other, and so much change? And moreover—how could the finite world emerge from the Infinite God?
    Cordovero's answer was:
    It is wrong to put such questions. It is wrong to imagine

God on one side and the world on the other side. It is wrong to imagine God and the world as two separate things. Echod—One Unity, that is the great secret of all and everything. One God and He contains in Himself all and everything, and everything is embraced under one law. God and world, God and His Creation is One. Spirit is bound up with matter and matter is bound up with spirit. The created is a new appearance only to the created, not to the Creator. For everything created was from all eternity, without end, without cessation, and without change, in God's thought. And thought is tantamount, is equal to existence. Divine Thought is the secret of existence. There is no existence outside God, and certainly not without Him. He is in all and outside all, but nothing is outside Him. God is the place of the world, but He Himself is in no place. He is all. All comes from Him, and there is no thing that is void of Him. Therefore—God and the world are One. And consequently, it is impossible to divide existence into finite and infinite. As God's Unity contains in itself the whole multitude of the world, so the Infinite contains the finite. And so, too, the changeable has no existence in the eternal changeless. It means all the worlds, the upper and the lower worlds, are one. It is all like a ladder, and the whole Creation, from the highest of all worlds to the lowest, and all the spheres (Sephirot) from the highest to the lowest, are only rungs of the ladder.

This is the only way in which we can understand the great mystery of God and His Creation, Cordovero said. He added: "Whoever was privileged to comprehend this in its full sense and meaning, and has seen behind the veil must never speak of it." Because human language has no words for it, human imagination has no symbolic image for it, and human understanding has no expression for it.

Rabbi Moses Cordovero stresses the complete similarity and likeness of being conscious and being, and he draws a logical conclusion that the real and the ideal—what is and should be, are one and the same.

He says:

"The Creator's knowledge is fundamentally different from man's knowledge, or the knowledge of any other created thing, for their knowledge, what they have come to know, is altogether different and distinct from the Knower. It means there is a certain barrier between the knowledge, the Knower and the known. In other words—between the thought, the thinker and what is thought about.

"It is quite different with the Creator—He is at one and the same time the knowledge, the Knower and what is known, all in one. For His knowledge does not consist of His discovering something that exists outside Him—He discovers and knows only Himself. And discovering Himself He thereby knows everything that exists, since nothing exists outside Him—everything is found in Him. He is the archetype of everything that exists. Everything rests in Him, in its highest and purest form, and the perfection of every existing thing consists indeed of this, that it becomes united with the Prime Source of all there is—and the more remote it grows from it, the further it is from perfection."

RABBI ISAAC LURIA—THE ARI

THE ARI'S system embraced both the Theoretical Kabbala and the Practical Kabbala.

Theoretically he saw the created world and the order of the world in a way very similar to Cordovero's system. His system is not so deep and rational, but it is richer in imagery. According to the Ari, before God created the world, the Infinite (En-Sof) filled the whole of infinite space. When God came to create the world, so that His (the Infinite's) attributes should emerge and manifest themselves and develop their perfection, space was needed for this innovation. What did God do? He concentrated Himself, contracted, shrank into Himself. And that produced an Infinite Light which filled the space vacated by the Glory of God. Then the Infinite Light also contracted and concentrated itself and left an empty space. That space became encompassed by Ten Circles (Vessels or Sephirot). Through their medium the endless number of creatures, the whole Creation, animate and inanimate, could emerge in all their incalculable diverse and separate forms.

But their diversities are only an illusory appearance, without which the human understanding could not comprehend it. The finite has no separate existence outside the Infinite. And, as already said, the Infinite Light had contracted to provide space for the Creation.

But this empty space, too, did not stay void of the Infinite Light. As a thin light-channel, the Infinite Light streams through all the circles (or vessels, or Sephirot) and penetrates into the area of Creation, meaning the world, the universe.

The first three outer circles were able to bear the Infinite Light, because they were nearer to the Infinite, to the En-Sof, and their substance was, therefore, purer than that of the other circles, the other Sephirot. These were not, however, able to bear the Infinite Light, and they burst. They therefore had to be removed as broken vessels from the central source of Light, and all the Sephirot had to be recreated. New Circle Faces (Parzufim) were created instead, in such a way that all the Parzufim (figures) taken all together, are in essence as one family—some are active masculine Parzufim, in the manner of "Father" (Abba); the others are passive, feminine Parzufim, in the manner of "Mother" (Imma).

There were also created what may be called the neutral Parzufim, in the manner of sons or daughters. Each Parzuf with its own soul.

In this regard of souls, they were created as part of the creation of the First Adam, and each one of them is a spark of the First Adam. All the souls when they were created, were entirely good, and so they remained till Adam's sin. When Adam sinned, a confusion set in between the Infinite Light—the Source of Absolute Good, and the broken vessels—the source of Absolute Evil. This confusion produced the present condition in the world, when there is nothing completely innocent and nothing completely guilty. There are in the holy souls, smoldering sparks of evil, of defilement, and in the evil souls there are hidden sparks of good. It is this state of neither one thing nor the other, that prevents Messiah from coming. For, as our sages said, Messiah cannot come otherwise than in a generation that is wholly just, wholly clean, innocent, or in a generation that is wholly unjust, wholly guilty. This means, as the Ari interpreted it— Messiah can only come when evil and corruption will be completely rooted out, extirpated by holiness, and the souls will be purified right through.

The souls keep longing and yearning for this to happen. As long as the soul is not purified it suffers great pain, and longs for improvement. To make the pain bearable, the soul is reincarnated in various evil people, even in animals and beasts. It also happens that an unpurified soul is reincarnated in a purified person, so as to be purified through him. The contrary, too, may happen, that a purified soul enters as a Dybbuk into an unpurified person, in order to purify his soul. And it can also happen that a man becomes pregnant (as the Kabbala puts it) with three or four souls at once— because they all want to be purified through him.

The Jews have a special mission in this. They are in exile to improve and to save the souls of other nations. Every Jew is, therefore, required to realize that he is under an obligation to strive for one purpose—to reform and save the world, the souls of the world.

How is this to be done?

Here the Ari puts forward his Practical Kabbala.

The souls of the world can be saved, he says, by mortification, by self-torment, by breaking down the desires of the flesh, by not eating, not sleeping, not enjoying life, by doing penance, constant penance for the sins one has committed, by solitude, by union with God—also by immersion in water, by cleansing oneself of sin, and by prayer according to specified forms (the Ari's form of prayer). And especially by observing scrupulously all the commandments, both those which were given in writing (the Torah) and those that were handed down by word of mouth (the Talmud). All these combined, constitute the practical methods through which to save one's own soul and the souls of the world, so as to bring down the Messiah and lead mankind to perfect salvation.

TWILIGHT UNDER
DARKENING SKIES

THE CURE BEFORE AFFLICTION

*T*HE MESSIANIC idea is firmly planted in the Jewish mind through the popular Jewish belief in ultimate good. This belief has sustained the Jewish people through all the trials, sufferings and calamities it has endured in the two thousand years of its history in Exile and Dispersion. The Bible calls the Jews a stiff-necked people. It is also an optimistic, deeply believing people.

There is a Jewish saying that God provides the cure before the affliction. This belief is the moral that is interwoven into all the Jewish folk-tales and legends revolving round good and evil, life and death, existence and non-existence—both in the mystic sense of these contraries and in their practical reality. This belief runs like a thread through the most primitive Jewish stories and legends beginning with Genesis, with the story of the Creation and even earlier. As for instance: God determined, God willed to create the earth and to create man upon it. In limitless, boundless space, Infinity, God decided to draw boundaries, to set limits. But the very idea of limitation, of boundaries, implies the corollary—beginning necessitates end. Immediately God laid the foundation of existence, its contrary, non-existence, followed. For just as there is the transition from Infinity to the finite, so there is also the contrary road, from the finite to Infinity. And both transitions involve pain and suffering—the pangs of birth and the pangs of death. For implicit in God's creation of the world, in the very act of creation, is its corollary, the great contradiction—*good* and *evil*—the good of being and evil of not-being, accompanied by the pangs of coming into being and of ceasing to be.

How could God do this? God who is Absolute, Positive, how could He permit such an act of Creation which by the very act itself, laid the foundation simultaneously for the negative—evil?

A hard question. But the Kabbalists have a complete answer—true, the evil was created, but before it was, God had already created the cure. The cure for the trouble is the *Torah*, which is the salve to heal all the evil in the world, the answer to all questions, the resolver of all doubts, the revelation of all mysteries, the ultimate blessing of all blessing, the good which is beyond all good. Before God created the world with all its curses, He had, much earlier—two thousand years earlier—created the Torah which should and which does heal all the wounds of the world, all the ills of existence in the world.

This is the position of Kabbala in relation to the whole conception of the world; it is also adapted to meet the different parts of this conception, including its special relationship to the sufferings of the Jewish people. For between good and evil, blessing and curse, much more has fallen to the Jewish lot on the negative side—more punishment than favor. Why? Where is the compensation, the recompense for all the sufferings? What good follows as the corollary of all this evil?

The Jewish faith has the answer to this question too—there is a preordained reward for the sufferings. The Jewish sufferings began with the Joseph of the Bible, Jacob's favorite son. His lot was to be sold as a slave into Egypt. But his suffering was designed for a specific purpose—for later aggrandizement. He was afterwards elevated to the eminence of Viceroy of Egypt, in order to save the world, including his family, from death by famine. Later, when the entire people of Israel was enslaved in Egypt, it was again for the purpose of future elevation—the people purified by sufferings became privileged to receive the Torah at Mount Sinai, and to win the inheritance of the Land of Canaan, which had been promised to Abraham. It was always the same, till the Destruction of the Second Temple. Whenever there was punishment, it was always for recompense, reward—if not physical, then spiritual, which is of even higher esteem.

In all the shadows the Kabbalists looked to find the hidden light, the silver lining in black clouds; as for the silver, it made no difference how little there was, if they could but find the answer to the darkness. For light is so precious and immeasurable, that even one ray of light redeems any amount of darkness.

How could the Jewish people justify the destruction of the Temple, the vast Jewish tragedy, the enormous number of victims, and the dispersion of the nation that followed, with all the sufferings prepared for it in Exile? Hard to answer that question. Yet the Jewish Agada answered it: *On the day the Temple was destroyed, that same day the Messiah was born.*

Only in order to be worthy to receive Messiah, the Jewish people must be thoroughly purified. One cannot profane the ideal, perfect purity with minds and hearts that are not correspondingly elevated, that are gross and not spiritual. Will a bridegroom sanctify his bride, under the marriage canopy, in his working clothes?

And this purification—is the birth pangs of Messiah. Wherever there are the pangs of sufferings they are interpreted as the sufferings of purification, the purification of the people preceding the coming of the pure Redeemer.

That is how the people interpreted the sufferings and the torments of the terrible period of Jewish martyrdom in Poland at the end of the 16th, and the beginning of the 17th century. The life of the Jews in Poland which had for centuries been comparatively favorable, became intolerable at the end of the 16th century. It was Poland, at the time of the Catholic reaction, which stifled the Reformation movement. The Jesuits who gained the mastery, set themselves the task of exterminating all heretics, and above all, the Jews, who "blasphemed Christ."

This reaction, as so often in Jewish history, led to a counter-reaction in Jewish life. The effort to destroy Judaism resulted in the counter-effort to strengthen Judaism.

And—Judaism in its deepest sense is *Kabbala*, the mystical orientation regarding the essence of being and not-being, finding a privilege in suffering, that the curse holds concealed the blessing of purification for the sake of the ultimate good. So the more the Church in Poland forced the Jews into a state of rightlessness, the more the Jewish people sought protection behind the fortified walls of Kabbala.

Kabbala has a twofold significance, both closely allied: Kabbala as a national conception, and Kabbala as a world concept. And these twin relationships exercise a daily mutual influence on each other, and are not to be parted. They flow together in one stream—the Kabbala as the mystical faith of an all-nations, all-human and even cosmic world-conception, and the Kabbala of tradition, sanctified by the belief that it goes far back into the past, right back to Moses, and is concerned with the welfare of the Jewish people, with the added conviction that this people is chosen to bring universal Redemption, the redemption of all peoples on earth.

This universal-national Redemption-dream of the Kabbalists has always dominated Jewish thought. The mystical tug at the soul, with all its various interpretations, has always held the minds of the noblest spirits among the Jewish people, and has directly influenced the course of Jewish life.

About the time of the anti-Jewish reaction in Poland, Polish Jewry had taken to the "Practical Kabbala" of the Ari, which is full of Messianic longing and hope. It opened to Jewish minds terrorized by the oppression of Church and State, the wonderful dream of Redemption, when the whole world would be pure and good and worthy of redemption from the forces of evil that held it captive. When this time would come, the long awaited True Redeemer, the Messiah, would appear.

The Messianic **Kabbala** became firmly planted in the hearts and minds of the Jewish people. Jews rose from their beds at midnight, full of faith, and sat on the floor and wept, lamenting the destruction of the Temple and the exile of the Shechina and the dispersion of the people of Israel. They prayed with broken hearts for the coming of the Redemption and the Restoration of the Tent of David.

Of course, the Jewish people at large did not and could not interpret Kabbala at that time in the profound sense of the authors of the Zohar and the other deeply speculative Kabbalists like Cordovero or Ari. These Kabbalists were possessed by a Holy Spirit which opened for them a vision to which it is hard to find anything equal in all world-literature, not even in Dante or Milton. They have nothing like the fantastic visions of the Kabbala explaining God's loftiness and infinitude, and uniting man with the Divine, and so making his soul immortal as the Divine essence is immortal.

Isaiah Horowitz— The "Shelah Ha-Kodesh"

The spiritual visionary Kabbala of the highest poetic ecstasy was beyond the understanding of the ordinary people. Even the scholars, the choice spirits, could not penetrate its

depths. The rabbis themselves conceived Kabbala more as
an intellectual exercise than as exalted poetic vision border-
ing on prophecy, and they argued and debated and split
hairs about its meaning, import and significance to such an
extent that the poetry completely escaped, leaving behind
only the superstition.

It was at the end of the 16th century that there arose in
Poland the great and profound Kabbalist, Isaiah Horowitz,
who brought the crown of Kabbala back to Poland. He was
born around 1655 and he is generally known as "Shelah ha-
Kodesh", Shelah being the initials of his principal work
SHENE LUCHOT HA-BRITH—The Two Luchot, the two Tables of
the Law which God gave the people of Israel, the Covenant
between Him and them.

SHENE LUCHOT HA-BRITH is the most outstanding, the
most profound Kabbalistic work written in that period. It is
full of beautiful ethical aphorisms and shrewd philosophi-
cal-theological observations, mystical pathos and exaltation.
Like a true giant of thought Horowitz is extremely modest,
and we find this modesty expressed in the Foreword to the
book. Everything expressed there, he tells us, is not his own
original thought—he only wanted to uncover "a fraction of
the fraction" that he had taken from writers and books following the road of the Zohar. He follows the road of the Ari.
He piles difficulties upon difficulties, but all in the spirit of
Kabbala. He turns each mitzvah into a mystery, finding a
deeper significance in it, a sacred symbol in each commandment of the Torah, something that "no son of man is able to
penetrate, even if he should live a thousand years."

In line with the Zohar, Isaiah Horowitz saw a hidden
mystic power not only in the mitzvoth themselves, but even
in the letters composing the words of the Torah. As for the
mitzvoth themselves, he discovered in them the symbols of
cosmic events. "The letters," he says, "conceal spirituality
in their shapes and in the numbers they add up to." He saw

"great wonderful secrets" not only in the Torah, but also in the Talmud.

According to the trend established by Isaiah Horowitz, all ethical problems, all obligations between man and man and man and God, derive from two foundations, Love and Holiness.

A man must never bear enmity in his heart against any other man. "You must never accuse your friend, neither in thought, nor in word, nor in act," is the teaching of the Shelah. And he expounds it in the following way:

"The Torah says, Love your neighbor like yourself. It means that what is dear and precious to you, do it also to your neighbor. If anyone has sinned against you, forgive him immediately. The whole community is one body, and will one hand strike the other hand?"

"The whole world," says the Shelah, "stands on this commandment, 'Love your neighbor'. Through his love for his fellow, man attains to the love of God, for both loves flow together into the Divine Unity."

"And God cannot be served in any other way than through love. We must love God not for the sake of any reward. Nor because of the fear of punishment. But only through 'inmost love,' through great longing and desire, through deep, intense, passionate, devouring, everlasting love." And Isaiah Horowitz keeps repeating over and over again that "the essential purpose and goal of man is to rise to the sublimity of God and to unite with Him."

Isaiah Horowitz emphasizes, all the time, the immensely important part of man in the whole scheme of the world— not only on this earth, but even in the vast space of the cosmos. The whole world, he says, exists only through and for the sake of man. Man is higher even than the angels. The angel has been created only out of good, and he cannot be other than good, for he has no free will. He does good only because he does not choose between good and evil. He does good only because he is incapable of doing evil. It is different with man. The good in man is the result of his overcoming evil, his victory in the ceaseless struggle between good and evil.

And suffering, Isaiah Horowitz tells us, is not a curse, but a blessing. For it is only through suffering, through constant unyielding war against evil, that man rises high. Man, through his actions, through his striving towards good, influences even the "upper worlds". Man's spirit is formed in the image of God; and this creates a bond between man and the Almighty, "as with a suspended chain, whose lowest links which drag over the earth, affect the links that are high up."

In this way, Isaiah Horowitz pursues the line of Kabbala, which denies the belief in the duality of good and evil, the belief that one derives from God and the other from some independent being. In the beginning, he teaches, there was only good, and the world was filled with undarkened light. Evil existed only as a potential, not actually effective. But through the sin of Adam and Eve, when they allowed themselves to be led astray by the serpent, evil passed from the potential to the actual, became real. Through the sin with which Adam and Eve were stained, the human spirit was converted into grossness, into uncleanliness, and evil became intermingled with good. Thus the harmony of the order of the world was upset.

But man can restore the harmony, can bring it back to its original unstained and unspotted splendor; he can do it through leading a clean and holy life. Then the rule of absolute and perfect good and light will be restored on earth, and the Messianic order will be established.

Man must remember it always, never forget it, never let it escape his mind. He must keep his life holy and must make every effort to beautify it with Divine Light. "My children," says the Shelah, "always, day and night, do not cease to think how to increase the holiness and the nearness to God." "Man must be holy with every step he takes, with every limb. He must consider his ten fingers as the symbol of the Ten Sephirot. Man's heart is in the likeness of the Holy of Holies. His mind is a spark of the world-wisdom. Man's every step and tread, all he thinks and does must be sanctified by the God-idea, so that he should be privileged to reach the height of 'God's Tent', where the Shechina rests."

We should note in this connection, the attitude which the Shelah, this great saint, takes in the matter if sexual intercourse. In rabbinical literature, it is regarded as the mitzvah of "increase and multiply." But the Shelah considers it not as an exegist, but as a mystic. Like all the Kabbalists, he sees the union of man and woman as a profoundly ethical and mystic symbol: through the union of the two sexes, man reaches a stage of Divine creation, which—the creation—came about through the pairing, which is essentially in the nature of the Divine. Sexual desire, the source of being and becoming, is in the Shelah's approach, purified and enveloped in a mantle of holiness. "Among all the holiness," he says, "there is nothing so holy to compare to the holiness of the sexual pairing." The union of man and wife is the image of the great mystery of becoming and being, the union of the Sephirot which are also divided in male and female, and they too join in union and so bring about Creation.

But Shelah's main preoccupation was why there was so much suffering inflicted on the Chosen people, the people that God, Himself, had chosen to bear His Name. His answer was that sufferings lead to greatness, sufferings purify, clear away the forces of evil. It is there that he sees the mission of Israel, the power of Redemption that is woven into its sufferings. "This lamb among the wolves," he says, speaking of Israel's road of martyrdom, "will lead the world to the true source of light, when all evil will cease and the world will be all-good. Soon, very soon," he encourages us, "there will come Messiah, the Redeemer, and justice and righteousness will rule the whole earth. God is One and His Name is One!"

There was little that Shelah revealed in Kabbala that was new. He started no trend of his own. He was only a follower and a popularizer of the ideas that are expressed in the Zohar and by the later Kabbalists, especially the Ari and his disciples. Yet, Isaiah Horowitz, the Shelah, did succeed in adapting the wonderful world of Kabbala to the particular spiritual climate of Polish Jewry. He found the right tone, the proper speech, the warm-hearted approach to strengthen the hopes, to deepen the faith and to enrich the dreams of the Jews in their Polish homes, where they were surrounded by hate and murder.

A little later, when the terrible catastrophe of the Chmielnicki massacres descended upon Polish Jewry, the Shelah became its favorite book. The remnants, the survivors of the massacres found in the Shelah hope and trust, the true salve for healing their wounds. They spoke of him with reverence and love by the name of his book—the Shelah ha-Kodesh, they called him, the holy Shelah, Isaiah Horowitz, who wrote SHENE LUCHOT HA-BRITH—THE TWO TABLES OF THE LAW or THE COVENANT, whose initials form the word SHELAH.

THE CHMIELNICKI MASSACRES

THE KABBALISTS had placed great hopes in the year Tov-Chet (1648), believing it would be the foretold fateful year when Messiah would come. They based their belief on a passage in the Zohar that in the year Tov-Chet (5408) all who lie underground would rise up and live, for it says (Leviticus 25:-13) "In the year of jubilee you shall return to every man his possession." Now the Gematria, the numerical value of the Hebrew word Zot, which means "this", is equal to Tov-

Chet, 5408. This led the Kabbalists to teach that the year 5408 would see the coming of Messiah. Instead, 5408 was the year of the most terrible massacres of Jews under the Cossack chieftain Bogdan Chmielnicki. (5408, in the Hebrew calendar, corresponds to 1648 A.D.)

In the Spring of that year, Chmielnicki became the Cossack Hetman, and started the Cossack rising against Poland, who then ruled the Ukraine, where the Cossacks lived. The rising was against Poland and the Poles, but the worst sufferings were inflicted on the Jews. The Jews had an alien religion, and they were mostly the administrators, the bailiffs, the innkeepers, the tax collectors employed by the Polish landowners. So all the Jews were proclaimed enemies, and wherever the Cossacks marched, they burned down Jewish homes and put Jews to the sword. 700 Jewish places of habitation were destroyed by fire and the estimates of the Jewish dead ran into the hundreds of thousands. Some placed them as high as 300,000.

Nathan Notte Hanover, the chronicler of those days, has described the terrible things that happened. Jews were flayed alive, they were mutilated, hands and legs chopped off and they were left to die. Women and children were ripped open. The chapter of horrors is too terrible for words.

But Nathan Notte Hanover also describes the heroism with which many Jews met their death. In Tulchin, the Poles betrayed the Jews to the Cossacks to save themselves. "The Jews outnumbered the Poles and could have overcome them, but Rabbi Aaron, head of the Yeshiva arose," relates Hanover, "and said: 'Hear me, my brothers! We are in exile among alien peoples. If you fall upon the Poles, other countries will hear of it and will take revenge on our brothers there. If this is a punishment from heaven, we must accept it and leave it to God.'"

And Nathan Notte Hanover further tells us that the entire Jewish population of Tulchin, numbering fifteen hundred souls, were shut up in a park. There were three rabbis with them, who exhorted them to die for His Name's Sake, and not forswear their faith. And they all cried "Hear O Israel, the Lord our God is One!" The Jews were kept shut up there for three days.

"Then a Cossack herald came, carrying a flag. He stuck the flag-pole in the ground, and cried aloud: 'Those who will accept the Christian faith will live!' Not one Jew answered. The herald repeated his message three times. The Jews all remained silent. Then the Cossacks entered and slew everyone with brutal savagery, including the three rabbis."

Jews fled from the small towns and villages to seek refuge in the fortified cities. The same fate overtook them. Several thousand Jews organized a strong defense in the walled and fortified town, Niemirov. The Cossacks, knowing they could not take the town in straight fight, adopted a ruse. They marched with the Polish banners, making the Jews believe that a Polish army had come to their rescue. The Jews opened the gates to them. And a savage massacre followed. Six thousand Jews, men, women and children, were killed. Many Jews jumped into the river to swim to the other shore, but the Cossacks shot them as they swam, and the waters were red with blood.

The Rabbi and Yeshiva head of Niemirov, Yechiel-Meir ben Eliezer, pleaded with the Jews not to yield to the temptation to save their lives by turning Christian. He was himself killed by the pogromists. He had hidden in the Jewish cemetery with his aged mother, thinking that if he was killed there, he would have Jewish burial. A Ukrainian resident of Niemirov saw him there and fell upon him. The old mother begged the murderer to kill her first, that she should not see her son's death. But he would not listen, and he killed the son before her eyes, and then he killed her.

Many young women who fell into the hands of the Cossacks killed themselves rather than be baptized and made their wives. The chronicles tell of many such. A Jewish girl being led away by a Cossack pretended she loved him and wanted to be his true wife. She said his life was so valuable to her that she would teach him a Jewish spell which made bullets harmless. To prove its effectiveness, she asked him to shoot her and he would see the bullet would bounce off harmlessly. When he shot her she fell dead.

The great Rabbi Shachna Cohen (Shach), another chronicler of the time, describes vividly the destruction of many Polish Jewish communities. "The band surrounded them, " he writes, recording the destruction of the Jewish community of Homel, "took everything they had from them, leaving them naked and bare, like sheep for the slaughter. Then these miscreants spoke to them gently: 'Why should you perish, why should you let yourselves be slain for your God, who has not pity for you? Come and serve our gods and our people. Then we will all live together. We will let you go free, and we will give you back all your possessions. You will live here like lords.' But the true servants of the Holy Seed," the Shach continued, "who always sacrificed themselves for his dear Name's Sake, rejected the delights of this world. Young and old, youths and maidens, ancients and innocent young children, all cried aloud their bitter cry to God who dwells on high—'One Sole God, King of all worlds! For Your Holy Name we give our lives—we shall not serve strange gods!' They confessed their sins, and with a great lamentation repeated penitential prayers. Then those inhuman creatures fell upon them savagely, without pity, and slew young and old, sons and daughters, all without exception."

We can measure the extent of the catastrophe by the large number of penitential prayers composed at that time, prayers in which the people poured their hearts out to God. Famous rabbis write these prayers, and they were read out in the synagogues on the Fast Day set to commemorate the new *Churban*, 20 Sivan.

They came to the heavenly Tribunal to cry out with horror against these bestial crimes. One of the prayers, "These Things I Shall Remember," composed by Rabbi Yom Tov Lipman Heller, calls these massacres the worst in the history of the Jews in the Dispersion. Another, Selicha, "When I Was in the House of the Lord," composed by Rabbi Sheftel Horowitz, calls it the Third *Churban*. "Why," the rabbi asks God, "why did our Father in Heaven decree this evil, the destruction of His people, to happen now, in Sivan, the month of the giving of the Torah, for which they are killing us?"

There is bewilderment in these prayers, bewilderment that this slaughter happened in the very year when it had been foretold that Messiah would come. Thus the Shach:

"The year Tov-Chet of the Sixth Thousand,
When I was preparing to go free."

But the *Churban* did not destroy the Messianic dream. The upheaval was too great for the dream to cease. On the contrary, it strengthened the longing for the Messiah.

The fact that this year to which they had looked forward hopefully had turned out so disastrously, only made the Kabbalists explain that it meant the Messiah was near. The Kabbala had always said that the Redemption would be preceded by violence and bloodshed—the wars of Gog and Magog, the birth-pangs of the Messianic age. These Jewish massacres were the first birth-pangs of that age from which the Jews would emerge purified and redeemed.

This faith—the very need of such a faith—spread throughout the length and breadth of the Jewish world. This, it was said, was the hour when Messiah would come. It grew to be a conviction that took possession of all the Jewish communities to the uttermost corners of the Jewish Dispersion, in Germany, Italy, Turkey and in Holland among the secret Jews who had escaped from the Inquisition in Spain and Portugal. The time was ripe for the new Messianic movement. Ten years after the *Churban* in the Ukraine, Poland and Lithuania, Shabbatai Zevi arose.

MENASSEH BEN ISRAEL
AND ABRAHAM HERRERA

THE PRACTICAL Kabbala of the Ari not only captured the hearts and minds of Polish Jewry, it also struck deep roots in Sephardic Jewry. It spread to every corner of the Jewish Dispersion. It won followers in Italy, and it spread to the new Jewish center in Holland.

In the first half of the 16th century, Italy was the only refuge for the Marranos to hide from the Spanish-Portuguese Inquisition. When the Catholic reaction spread also to Italy, the Marranos found a new refuge in Holland, which had, after a heroic war, won independence from Spain, and became a bulwark of freedom and tolerance. By the end of the 16th century, Marranos were arriving in Holland from Spain, Portugal and Italy, and in a decade or two, a rich and flourishing Jewish life had grown up, with its center in Amsterdam. And these refugees, these people in flight from persecution and death, helped to develop trade and industry in their new homeland, and helped Holland to become a dominant Power in the markets of the world.

The Marranos brought to Holland, not only material wealth, but also cultural treasures. There were among the Marranos, doctors, scientists, scholars, writers, poets. They opened schools, academies, and libraries and soon Amsterdam was one of the most important Jewish cultural centers in Western Europe.

The Jews in Amsterdam found in the religious freedom and tolerance that obtained in Holland a stimulus towards closer contact with general European learning. They had, after all, been brought up in the dogmas of the Catholic Church, had busied themselves with theological speculation and mystic thought, and had finally, as a result, rejected the faith in which they had been brought up and educated. It had developed in them a critical approach, a spirit of enquiry, that could not be satisfied with accepted tradition. It explains how Amsterdam Jewry, at that time, produced a skeptic like Uriel Acosta and an independent thinker like Spinoza.

At the same time the Catholic Faith which the Marranos had rejected, had left a definite religious impress on their minds. They remained religious believers. They were dedicated heart and soul to the Jewish religion for which they had sacrificed so much, and for which so many of their close kin had died. They were animated with the proud dream of a universal Jewish mission, and the mystical teachings of Kabbala found a ready reception and acceptance among them.

The Messianic ideal that was spread around that time by the Marrano Shlomo Molcho, who was afterwards martyred for it, came like a magic call to the Marrano refugees in Holland, many of whom had escaped from the dungeons of the Inquisition and the expectation of death at the stake in one of the many autos da fe, in which their nearest relatives, their parents, their brothers and sisters had perished. They had witnessed to their Judaism with their blood. And these Marranos, highly educated as they were in universal knowledge, with a good grounding in philosophical studies, were nevertheless also imbued with mystical ideas. There were two great teachers in that Amsterdam environment—Manasseh ben Israel and Abraham (Alonzo) Herrera.

Jewish history knows Manasseh ben Israel as the man who intervened with Cromwell to secure the readmission of Jews to England. But he was also an important writer, a scholar, a thinker, a man with great rabbinic and philosophical knowledge. He knew Latin as well as he knew Hebrew, and he knew equally well a number of European languages, above all Spanish. He claimed to know ten languages, including English. His great work is EL CONCILIADOR (The Conciliator) in Spanish, said to be the first work written by a Jew, in a modern language which had an independent interest for Christian readers. He corresponded with the greatest scholars of his age, among them Grotius. He explained in "El Conciliador", which runs to four volumes, the seeming inconsistencies of some passages in the Bible, and reconciles them.

The approaching year 1666 was looked upon by Christian theologians as the apocalyptic year, the year of wonders, in which the heavens would open and the Kingdom of Heaven would appear in all its glory. These mystic expectations coincided with the Manasseh ben Israel's strong Messianic ideas. He was oppressed by the sufferings of the Jewish people. In Germany, the Jews were being persecuted. In Spain and Portugal, Jews were being burned in the autos da fe. In Poland, the Jews were massacred by the Chmielnicki Cossacks. Manasseh ben Israel was convinced that these were all the birth pangs of the Messiah and that out of this darkness, the light of Redemption would suddenly blaze forth. He searched the Kabbala to discover when Messiah would come. And he concluded that he was already on the way, that Redemption would be soon.

Abraham Herrera was pursuing the same course. He, too, searched the Kabbala, and was sure that the Redemption was near.

Abraham Herrera had not only Jewish blood; he also had ancient Spanish blood, being descended from Gonzalo de Cordova, conqueror and viceroy of Naples. He had held high office in the Royal Court in Spain He was already a man of middle age when he left Spain and went to Amsterdam, where he declared himself of the Jewish faith. We do not know what had led him to this step. He was a serious thinker, with a good philosophical training. He was a Neo-Platonist. It led him to seek affinities with Neo-Platonism in the Kabbala. In his book THE GATE OF HEAVEN, which he wrote in Hebrew, he says: "As Rabbi Moses Cordovero employs philosophical methods to establish the truth of Kabbala, so I, too, employ the philosophy of Plato and his followers to show how right Kabbala is."

Herrera's great achievement is that he brought order and clarity into the Kabbala of the Ari. He explained the Ari's interpretation of the multifariousness of *Being*.

The Creation of the world was achieved by the one single emanation of the En-Sof (the Infinite) that the Ari names "Adam Kadmon," original man—the original form of man, which is also the hidden Divine idea. This first and most complete emanation is the Cause of all subsequent causes, the creative force in the Act of Creation, of *Becoming* and *Being*. This emanation is also the first name of the En-Sof, for the En-Sof Himself has no Name. He is without bounds, limitless, and cannot, therefore, be confined in a name—He is above all names.

In connection with this single, sole emanation of the En-Sof, Adam Kadmon, Herrera draws a comparison between Heavenly Man and Earth Man. As the Earth Man surpasses in perfection all other creatures in the world, being the pattern and final purpose of the whole Creation, so the Heavenly Man is superior to and more perfect than all other emanations and Heavenly Powers, of which he, the Heavenly Man, is the source and the Beginning. The Earth Man is the focus that takes in all the sanctified points of the Shechina—He spreads and irradiates Holiness throughout the world. The Earth Man is the reflection of the Light that was absorbed, and strives towards the heights to its original source. The Heavenly is the actual source of Light, that shines upon and animates all.

The Earth Man raises, elevates all to the First Cause, and the Heavenly Man who is an emanation of the First Cause, unites and embraces all degrees, from the highest to the lowest. The Earth Man is the spot on which the *Shechina* rests, the Tent of the Heavenly Kingdom. And the Heavenly is the Tabernacle, the Holy Temple of the En-Sof.

This brings Herrera to the Messianic idea: The Supreme Representative, the highest expression, the profoundest depth of the Earth Man, what is concealed in him of the Heavenly Kingdom—is the Bright Messiah, the Redeemer of the world, who will wipe away the dross from man, will cleanse him from pollution and sin, liberate him from the vale of tears, and lift him to the heavenly heights, to the source of endless Light, to the very source of the *Shechina*.

AT THIS time, when Manasseh ben Israel and Abraham Herrera published their Kabbala works announcing the speedy coming of the Redemption, life throughout the Jewish Dispersion kept growing darker and more bitter. The Jewish people suffered terribly, and their only hope was the speedy coming of the Redeemer, the coming of the Redemption, when these sufferings would end, and Messiah ben David would bring goodness and peace to the tormented nation.

But the Day of the Redemption did not come. On the contrary, the sufferings increased. In the very decade in which Manasseh ben Israel and Abraham Herrera published their works promising the Redemption, the worst torments and horrors were inflicted on the largest Jewish settlement, the Jews in Poland, the Chmielnicki pogroms in which 700 Jewish communities were destroyed and a quarter of a million Jews were slain.

The Jews all over the world were in despair. Something must happen, they said, to end this misery. So they turned to the prophecies of Manasseh ben Israel and of Herrera as offering them hope that the Redemption was at hand. They believed that God would at last hear their bitter cry and would save them.

At this fateful moment, the figure of a fantastic dreamer, an exalted mystic rose on the Jewish horizon, a man who had lost the faculty of distinguishing between the actual, the real and the imaginary, between dream and reality, a man whose soul was filled with the hopes and desires of his suffering fellow-Jews and throughout the Jewish Dispersion, the great message went out that the long-awaited had appeared, the Day of Judgment was at hand, and soon the Redemption would come. The Messiah was approaching with regal tread.

The people surrendered to him with complete blind faith, with ardent love. His name was Shabbatai Zevi, who proclaimed himself the True Messiah, Messiah ben David.

Shabbatai Zevi

The tragedy of the Shabbatai Zevi movement is presented in Jewish history as one of the tragedies of False Messianism. It was that, indeed. But the question remains whether Shabbatai Zevi set out deliberately to deceive.

The great Yiddish poet, Leivick, who devoted his genius to the Messianic idea, once said there were no False Messiahs. "All Messiahs were true; not False Messiahs, but Messiahs who failed. They had to fail in order to make room for a new one to come."

Shabbatati Zevi did not deliberately deceive. He was not an adventurer, but one who "failed". He was the Kabbalist who could not distinguish between reality and fantasy, between normal and abnormal. With his mystic flame he roused among the people the belief that their sufferings were the Messianic birth pangs, and that the day of Redemption had already come.

From his earliest youth, Shabbatai Zevi had given himself up to the study of the Ari's Kabbala. He afflicted his body, he fasted, so as to divest himself of the material and to enter the realm of the spirit. He lived at a time and in an environment full of Messianic beliefs and feelings, emotions and hopes, when people were anticipating trustfully the End of Days, when the bright Redeemer would come and put an end to the darkness on earth.

And now it was the year Tov-Chet which the Zohar indicated as the year of Redemption. But instead of Redemption the year had brought massacres and destruction at the hands of Chmielnicki's Cossack hordes. Shabbatai Zevi, like all the Kabbalists of his time, saw this terrible catastrophe as heralding the birth pangs of the bright Redeemer, who would soon reveal himself to the whole world.

Shabbatai's asceticism, his melodious voice, his magnetic presence, his eyes blazing with mystic fire, drew round him a band of enthusiastic followers and admirers, and they contributed to the misleading ideas ripening in his mind that he himself might be the favored one, the Chosen, the Redeemer for whom the soul of the people had longed and prayed. Perhaps he was, himself, indeed the Chosen one, the Redeemer.

He hinted at this intoxicating thought to those nearest to him, and they took up the idea rapturously and fortified him in the belief. and it happened! He, Shabbatai ben Mordecai Zevi, was the one for whom the People of Israel had waited this long time! He would redeem the People from their sufferings, would end their wanderings, and lead them back to the Promised Land of the Patriarchs! He would bring the Redemption!

It is outside our present scope to deal with the question of the Shabbatai Zevi movement as a whole. What we want to do is to indicate how passionately the Jewish people yearned for a Deliverer, a Redeemer, a great and wonderful man, a superman, who would fulfill all their dreams. And now the Jewish people could see in Shabbatai Zevi the concrete embodiment of their abstract ideas and hopes of Redemption and the Redeemer.

The message that Shabbatai Zevi was the True Messiah

spread like wildfire through all the places where Jews lived, and was received with frantic enthusiasm. Jewry was drunk with the news. The Messiah had come at last! The Redeemer was here! God had listened to their prayers! And He was sending them solace and recompense for their sufferings. A mad joy took hold of them. All sections of the Jewish People were infected by it—the simple folk masses and the intellectual giants of the age, great and renowned rabbis, tiny remote communities and large and important Jewish settlements in the big centers of the world. Wherever Jews dwelled, they gathered in the synagogues, the *batei midrash* and in the streets, and danced and sang—Messiah had come! Bands of Prophets formed everywhere, as in biblical days, and went about prophesying; men and women who felt the Spirit of God upon them, and proclaimed that Shabbatai Zevi was the Messiah.

Notwithstanding the difficulties and the dangers of the journey, people set out from near and far to make their way to the new Messiah, to see him and pay him homage. All Jewry stood eager and prepared for the march to the Land of Israel, to liberate it. Adherents flocked to Shabbatai Zevi. He won many devoted followers, and none more devoted than Nathan Ashkenazi Ghazzati, who became his "Prophet".

Nathan had seen terrible things happen to Jews in Europe, especially in Poland. He associated those Jewish sufferings with the ideas in Kabbala; he viewed them as a prelude to the coming of Messiah. He made his way to Palestine, to join Shabbatai there, and he proclaimed him in writings sent far and wide as the True Messiah. He said that he had on the night of Shavuoth, heard a voice from Heaven declare: "In a year and a few months from now, Messiah ben David will reveal himself." "You should know," Nathan circularized the Jewish communities, "that our Messiah was born in the town Izmir (Smyrna), and he calls himself by the name Shabbatai Zevi. He will soon reveal his Kingship before the whole world. He will take off the royal crown from the head of King Ishmael and will set it upon his own head. And the Sultan will follow him like an obedient slave, because the world belongs to him, to Shabbatai."

Nathan's "Prophecy" gained credence in all circles. People went delirious with joy. They gathered in crowds and sang Hallelujahs to the Messiah, Shabbatai. They followed him, crying: "Shabbatai Zevi is the True King Messiah!" Jews all over the world closed their businesses and went to follow Shabbatai.

Shabbatai's Scribe, Samuel Primo, sent letters to all Jewish communities in Asia, Africa, and Europe, announcing that the "Time of Miracles" had arrived, and that people should prepare for great events. The letters were written in the form of royal proclamations.

The movement grew. Reports went round that the entire People of Israel had risen and was moving towards the Land of Israel, led by holy men and by strong men, to liberate it from the Turks.

Glueckel Hamelin, who lived at that time in Hamburg, relates in her memoirs: "It's impossible to describe the joy that possessed us when we received the letters (from Turkey). Most of the letters came to the Sephardim, and Reach time the letters were brought to the synagogue and read out. The Ashkenazim came there as well, young and old. The young Portuguese (Sephardim) put on their best clothes, with a wide sash of green silk—Shabbatai Zevi's emblem. They went off to the synagogue with drums and cymbals, as once of old at the festival of the Drawing of Water, and they read out the letters that had been received. Others sold all their possessions, and waited day by day for the Redemption. My father-in-law, who lived in Hamelin, abandoned his house there with everything in it, and went to Hildesheim. From there he sent us two big barrels of linen and food—peas, beans, smoked meats, dried fruits and other things that will keep a long time. The good man reckoned that we would go straight from Hamburg to the Land of Israel. The barrels stood in my house for over a year. In the end my father-in-law was afraid the food would go bad. So he wrote to us to open the barrels and take out the food, so as not to spoil the linen. The barrels stayed there for three whole years, and my father-in-law still thought he would need them for the journey. But the Lord God had no wish to release us from the Exile."

Glueckel Hamelin has transmitted to us, here, the feeling that prevailed at that time among the Jewish folk masses and among the leaders of the big Jewish communities of Western Europe, Ashkenazim and Sephardim alike. Obviously this feeling was even more intense in Poland where the Jews had not yet recovered from the terrible massacres and destruction under Chmielnicki. The Messianic hope grew in Polish Jewry into a real mass movement. Jews abandoned their homes and possessions. They were sure that they would not need anything more. The Redemption had come. The Exile had ended! They would now go back to their own Jewish land and live there as free men.

But, as we know, the Shabbatai Zevi movement ended tragically. When the time came for Shabbatai Zevi to confront the Sultan and demand Palestine from him, his courage failed. He was not like Shlomo Molko, prepared to die as a martyr. He was not another Bar Kochba, to die heroically on the battlefield. He submitted to the Sultan and embraced the Islamic faith. And Jews all over the world tore their garments and mourned as for one who had died.

MESSIANISM AS A SPIRITUAL MOVEMENT

THE JEWISH people were sunk in despair. Their hopes of Redemption had miscarried. The spiritual blow of Shabbatai Zevi's conversion to Islam hit them as hard as the physical blow of the Chmielnicki pogroms. Jews began asking bitter questions. What was the good of their Judaism? Where was it leading them? Vanity of vanities! What was the use of anything?

But the despair did not last. The Jewish people shook it off. Their deep faith in God and His Judgment was not overthrown. It survived even this disastrous delusion. The deeply wounded soul of people did not cease to dream and to see visions. When the reality became too bitter, they turned for comfort to the "hidden vision", they sought healing in the Kabbala works of Isaiah Horowitz, Manasseh ben Israel, Abraham Herrera, and their like.

That saved the Jewish people. The world of reality having become a vale of tears, the Jewish people sought refuge in another world, a world of mystic dreams and fantastic visions. That mystical world became more real and more actual to them than the sad and painful reality.

Shabbatai Zevi had rocked and shaken the Jewish soul, had upset its whole balance. But the spirit of national political Redemption that he had evoked was not destroyed. When the Jewish people lost their hope in political Messianism they found solace in spiritual Messianism. New mystics arose in different corners of the Jewish Dispersion, who demanded that Jews should afflict their bodies, should fast and repent, in order to bring nearer the coming of the True Messiah. In spite of all the disappointments, indeed, because of them, and in spite of them, faith in the True Redeemer must not be abandoned. Though he may tarry, he would come! And fasting and repentance and prayer would hasten his coming!

After Shabbatai Zevi's apostasy it might have been expected that the Jewish people would turn away with revulsion from this illusion, and would denounce him as a traitor, a renegade, a blasphemer. But it did not happen like that. They had put too much hope and trust in the idea of the Messiah, they had wanted too much to believe in him. And the whole story of Shabbatai Zevi's apostasy seemed unbelievable. There were many Jews who dismissed it as a lie put out out by their enemies. They could not believe it. It was impossible!

Even when it became certain that the news of Shabbatai Zevi's apostasy was true, many Jews tried to find excuses and explanations. It was not the Messiah who had apostatized, they said, but a shadow, a phantom who had taken on his appearance. The True Shabbatai Zevi had ascended to Heaven and would soon return and reveal himself through fresh miracles. The Shabbatai Zevi legend took on the form of a Jesus Christ death and resurrection. In this way the belief in Shabbatai Zevi lingered on.

Shabbatai Zevi sects grew up in a number of Jewish communities, mostly in the Turkish provinces and in Italy. In Poland, too, many Jews continued to believe in Shabbatai Zevi for decades after his apostasy. Secret groups formed in a number of Polish towns and sent messengers to Salonica, which was the center of the Shabbatai Zevi movement, to discover all they could about the new faith. The messengers came back with the glad news that Messiah would soon reappear. He had suffered a temporary defeat because of the sins of the world, but he would finally triumph over them.

One of those who believed in Shabbatai Zevi's speedy return was the Kabbalist Chaim Malach, who established close contact with the leaders of the Shabbatai Zevi sect in Salonica. He conducted an active Shabbatai Zevi propaganda in Poland. Not openly, because the official Jewish leaders would have excommunicated him, but in small secret groups. He taught that Shabbatai Zevi was the True Messiah, and that Jews must repent, must mortify their flesh, and cleanse and purify themselves to clear the way for his return.

There was also Yehuda Chassid, mystic and ascetic, who preached to the Jewish communities in Poland on the lines of the Ari's Kabbala, that great miracles would soon occur, and Messiah would come. He did not mention Shabbatai

Zevi by name, but preached a Messianic hope as such, and he gathered round him a circle of "Chassidim" who endeavored by fasting and mortifying the flesh, to hasten the End of Days.

When the number of these "Chassidim" reached 1,500 souls, they set out with Yehuda Chassid and Chaim Malach at their head for Palestine, to welcome the Messiah there. They were bitterly disappointed. Messiah did not appear. They were plunged into despair. Yehuda Chassid took it to heart, and died a broken man. His "Chassidim" deprived of his inspiration and leadership, dispersed, and most of them drifted sadly one by one back to their old homes. Some joined the Shabbatai Zevi sect in Turkey, the Doenmeh, and became Moslems. Others who returned to Poland became Christians.

Chaim Malach stayed on for a while in Jerusalem, till the rabbis of the Holy Land drove him out. He returned to Poland and soon after died there.

It was not the end of the Shabbatai Zevi movement, however, neither in Poland nor in Italy nor elsewhere. But the rabbis and the leaders of the Jewish community opposed it bitterly, ostracizing everyone who was under the slightest suspicion of Shabbatai Zevi-ism. The hostility went so far that it extended to one of the brightest figures who appeared at that time in Italian Jewry, the poet and Kabbalist Moses Chaim Luzzatto.

MOSES CHAIM LUZZATTO

THE SHABBATAI ZEVI Messianic movement had its aftermath in Italian Jewry, partly because Italian Jews were largely engaged in sea-trading, which brought them in close contact with residents in the sea ports of Smyrna and Constantinople, where Shabbatai Zevi had established his centers. There had been a number of Italian rabbis among Shabbatai Zevi's most ardent followers, but after their disillusionment when he had apostatized, they became doubly zealous in trying to root out every suspicion of Shabbatai Zevi-ism and persecuted those who showed any signs of still adhering to the heresy. One of those on whom their hand fell heavily about twenty years after, was a man who had not the remotest connection with Shabbatai Zevi, Moses Chaim Luzzatto.

Luzzatto, born in Padua in 1707, developed an early talent for poetry. He knew Latin and Italian perfectly, and they influenced his Hebrew writing. He wrote a new Hebrew Psalter on the model of the Scriptural, and a Hebrew drama on the biblical theme of Samson and the Philistines. He was only 18 when he attracted attention with a Hebrew morality play MIDGAL OZ (The Tower of Strength), which is still considered one of the classics of modern Hebrew literature.

He tells the story in MIDGAL OZ of an ancient tower on a mountain peak, with a wonderful garden at the top of the tower. But the walls of the tower were smooth and slippery, so that no one could climb up the tower to reach the garden. Then the King of the land made a public proclamation that he would give his daughter in marriage to anyone who would climb the tower and open the way to the garden.

One day a Prince from a neighboring country rode past the tower. The Prince's name was Shalom. He hadn't heard of the King's proclamation, but his curiosity was roused by the tower. He explored it from all sides, looked carefully into every corner, and he found a tunnel under it, with a concealed door which led up to the garden. But as he didn't know of the King's proclamation, he did not claim the reward. Then a man named Zippe, a liar and a fraud, passed and saw the door which Shalom had left open. He rushed off to tell the King that he had discovered the way up to the garden. And according to his promise, the King gave Zippe his daughter, whose name was Shulamith, to be his bride. Not long after, Prince Shalom and Princess Shulamith met and fell in love. Now the true story of the discovery of the concealed door came out. Zippe confessed that he had lied. And Shalom married the Princess Shulamith.

But it is not because of the story that the MIGDAL OZ is famous, but for its simple and vigorous style, recalling that of the Bible, vastly different from the stilted artificial Hebrew style of his contemporaries.

Moses Chaim Luzzatto wanted, however, to be more than a poet. He delved into the mysteries of the Zohar, and he began to write in the style and the thought of the Zohar, producing a work that he called THE SECOND ZOHAR. He revealed his studies in Kabbala to a circle of his friends, and they were enthusiastic. Luzzatto himself couldn't believe that he was able to write a work so close in language and spirit and style to the Zohar; he convinced himself that it had come through a heavenly messenger, an angel dictating the words to him, telling him what to write. He spoke of this, too, to his circle of friends, and they were elated. They made him their rabbi, their teacher; they were sure that he would soon appear to the world, bringing a new Revelation.

But what his young friends hailed as a new revelation was considered by the persecuting rabbis as heresy, and they suspected Moses Chaim Luzzatto of being under the influence of the Shabbatai Zevi-ists. One of these rabbis, Moses Hagiz, who was in Altona, denounced Luzzatto and wrote to the rabbis in Padua, where Luzzatto lived, to suppress this new movement in its beginnings, "before it reaches the mass of the people."

The rabbis in Padua summoned Luzzatto and made him sign a statement that as long as he lived outside Palestine he would not engage in Kabbala study and would not write in the language of Kabbala.

Luzzatto returned to writing poetry. He wrote an allegorical drama, GLORY TO THE RIGHTEOUS, which gave a new modern direction to Hebrew poetry. It is on this account that

Luzzatto is called the "Father of Modern Hebrew Literature". He no longer tells a love story, with hymns to romantic love but he expresses profound thoughts with a beautiful diction—a wise and mature work. He explains that he is not trying to paint real living people, but to personify abstract ideas. It is all a *Mashal*, an allegory, a fable, a moral. Mashal appears in the Prologue as a person, and says that he has come forward only to serve wisdom, and it will not be he, Mashal, but Wisdom, who will speak to the audience, and implant in the hearts of the people the seeds of knowledge and admonition.

He introduces in the drama, the son of Truth, Justice, and his colleagues, Understanding, Folly, Pride, Falsehood, Patience. It is a morality play of high poetic order, a work that years have not staled.

Yet Luzzatto remained, at bottom, the Kabbalist. Poetry was a much lesser thing to him than Kabbala. The great poet thought little of his poetry because the problems of life and death, of God and the Creation and the after-life tormented him, and only the speculations of the Kabbala could compose his mind and spirit. Notwithstanding his promise to the rabbis, he continued to explore the realms of dream and mysticism. He felt himself surrounded by holy spirits. But since he had undertaken not to publish any Kabbalistic work, not to write of his own mystic visions, he compiled works of apologetics in which he spoke highly of the "secret wisdom." He wanted to show that only Kabbala and not rationalist philosophy could give the right answer to the problems of life and existence, the great mystery of the Will of the Prime Cause, which is beyond man's comprehension, which is endless and limitless, and which reveals its Will through the limited forms of the Sephirot, who are within the bounds of human understanding.

In these works, Luzzatto is again the master of a wonderfully clear and lucid style, through which he conveys the

most abstruse and complex philosophical-mystical arguments simply and understandably. He sets out there his
Kabbalistic ideas about the cosmic universal value of man.
In man's active deeds he reveals his Divine essence; the fate
of the world, of the universe, of the entire cosmos is concealed in the depths of the human soul; and the harmonious
perfection of the world consist of the fact that the general
law of the universe is at the same time the human law, the
revelation of the spirit of man, of his moral consciousness.
Man's moral conduct, his obedience to the commandments
of God's Torah, is a moral act of cosmic dimensions. The
highest pattern of life, the model and prototype of all Creation, is the spiritual image of man, his meaning and purpose as the reflection of God and man's stirring and striving
towards God. The world can flame with the light of the
Shechina only through the merit of illuminated man, reflect-
ing the Divine universal righteousness.

The watchful rabbis renewed their accusations against
Luzzatto charging that he was preaching heresy, propagat-
ing false Messianism. They demanded that he must not print
anything without their permission. He rejected this demand,
and the rabbis pronounced the ban against him.

Things became too difficult for Luzzatto where he was,
and he finally had to take up his wanderer's staff, and move
to Amsterdam, where the Sephardic community received
him with great honor. Wishing to be materially independent, he worked, like Spinoza before him, at polishing lens-
es and precious stones.

But still his spirit found no rest. In Amsterdam, too, he
could think only of the mysteries of Kabbala. He was convinced that in Kabbala there was concealed the wonderful
power with whose help he would be able to break the chains
of Messiah, redeem the whole world and end the sufferings
of the Jewish people. Luzzatto was also convinced that only
on the sacred soil of the Land of Israel would one penetrate

into the mysteries of Kabbala. Only there could one transmit the Kabbalistic wisdom and fulfill its purpose.

So Luzzatto went to realize his great desire, to tread the soil of the Holy Land. Like the great poet, Yehuda Halevi, before him, he set out on his long journey and he reached Safad, the town of Moses Cordovero and of the Ari. But death soon extinguished his hopes, and ended his labors. In the midst of his plans he was stricken by the plague and died, he and his wife and his son. He was only forty. But what he had been able to do in his short life, opened a new epoch in Hebrew poetry and in Jewish mystic thought.

HASIDISM—ITS ORIGIN AND MEANING

THE PROFUNDITIES OF KABBALA AND THE ORDINARY FOLK

*A*LL THE profound Kabbala speculations and meditations made no real impact on the great mass of the people, with the consequence that their soul was left poorer. For the Jewish spirit is actually inclined towards mysticism and God-seeking, the longing and desire for God. It is only because of the Dispersion, the Exile and the continuous wanderings, that the Jewish religion had to fence itself round with laws and strict commandments and observances which rationalized the religion. Yet time after time the true spirit of the people, its mystic soul wakens, and it rebels against the hardened religious dogmas and customs that destroy the soul of the faith. The Kabbala had little influence on the masses not because of any fault in the people, but because of the fault of the Kabbalists—they were all scholars, bookmen, saints, lofty spirits, but not leaders of the people, not teachers, not Prophets who could teach and influence the people. They sat in solitude, shut away, isolated in their studies, absorbed in their thoughts, writing their learned works. It is true that they sowed and planted their thoughts, but the harvests stayed between the covers of their books. They reached only the select few, individuals—they did not satisfy the hunger and still the thirst of the mass of the people. What the Kabbalists wanted the people to do was beyond the power of the ordinary folk. The Kabbalists expected the people to mortify and afflict themselves, to practice self-denial, to renounce life and the enjoyment of natural things. Most people can't do that. The Kabbalists thought the mass of the people could rise to their own height, but the mass of the people can't rise to that height. The people expected these great spirits, the redeemers, the saints to come down among them and speak to them in their own language, and when they failed to do that the people grew confused and wandered away from the path for a long time.

It was only with the coming of the Hasidic movement that the people at last obtained the spiritual nourishment which it sought.

Wʜᴀᴛ Wᴀs Nᴇᴡ ɪɴ Hᴀsɪᴅɪsᴍ

Wʜᴀᴛ ᴅɪᴅ Hasidism give the Jews? What new thing did it introduce into the Jewish religion, its ideas, observances and endeavors that it made such a tremendous impact on the Jewish people that they joined its ranks in hundreds of thousands and became its devoted followers, body and soul?

The answer is that Hasidism introduced, in fact, nothing new. Hasidism is not a new faith, nor is it a reform of the faith. Hasidism has renounced no fundamental principle of Judaism, has not permitted anything that traditional Judaism had forbidden. All the ideas that Hasidism advanced and defended and preached had already been expressed in a number of works, ancient and modern. All the ideas put forward by Hasidism, about God and the Creation, about man and his soul, about matter and spirit about the upper world and the lower, about the souls and the spirits that hover in space, all the demands that Hasidism imposes on man so that he should find union with God and the higher realms, all that Hasidism says about devotion in prayer, about contemplation, about ecstasy in the worship of God, about prayer, about joy in life—all these things are not new; they had found much earlier expression in mystical and moralistic Judaism.

Then what is there wonderful about the existence and the triumph of Hasidism? What is the hidden power that won so many hundreds of thousands of Jews?

The answer is that the power of Hasidism lies not in what it contains, but in its form. Hasidism found a way of establishing a synthesis between the two systems of Kabbala, the Theoretical and the Practical, and with a few changes it created a single whole on which it erected a complete way of life. The main point is that to Hasidism, Kabbala was not a literary synthesis but a way of life. Hasidism did not wait for the intellect of the people at large, as a whole, to develop to the stage when the people would be able to understand the theoretical attitudes of the Kabbala. Instead, it clothed itself in simplicity, and descended to the people, to the ordinary folk-masses, and nourished their simple faith in God and man. By this alone, by descending to the ordinary folk, Hasidism stimulated the mass of the people to recognize their own worth and to rise to the heights.

Hasidism also brought to the people the cult of the Rebbe, the Zaddik, as the intermediary between the people and God. The Zaddik, too, is himself a man of the people. He is not like the old Kabbalist, aloof, remote, isolated in his study, absorbed in his books and his meditations, quoting at every step chapter and verse from works of which the ordinary folk have no knowledge. The Zaddik, on the contrary, though spiritually exalted to the pitch of direct approach to God, is nevertheless part and parcel of the people, identified with them fully in their hopes and aspirations. He is the direct mediator between God and the Hasidism, the advocate, the special pleader, the interceder for the people of Israel.

Furthermore, the Hasidim freed the people from the dread that goes with strict God-fearing. They discarded the belief of the Practical Kabbala that to purify himself, man must mortify his flesh by fasting and self-denial. They saved Jewish souls from despair. Their teaching was the contrary of gloom—they taught that we must worship God with joy, and that only through gladness can we achieve purity of soul.

THE ESSENTIAL OF HASIDIC FAITH

THE ESSENTIAL of Hasidic faith is the principle of the Kabbala, as taught by Moses Cordovero, that the difference between the two worlds, the upper and the lower, is only external, and that both are in reality linked together and influence each other. The deep faith of the Kabbalists, including Moses Cordovero, that the world is only an emanation from God, and that matter and spirit are intermingled (sparks of holiness), found this definite expression in Hasidism—the Creator is always present in the Creation. Nature is only the garment of the Divine in which it has hidden from the eye of man. So it is man's duty to reveal the spiritual in the world.

The essential faith of Hasidism is founded on the declaration in the Kabbala: "There is no place where He (God) is not." On this basis the Hasidim come and teach the people:

Let man consider that all there is in the world is full of the Creator, Blessed be He! And that all things that are done on this earth by the power of man's thought are from God's

Providence, Praise His Name! Man must consider that the Creator fills the whole world, that His Glory and His Shechina are always with Him, and that He is the most absolute spirituality there can be, and He is the Lord of all creatures in the world, and He can do all that He wishes, and therefore it is good for a man to rely only on Him. Blessed be He!

The Hasidim teach further:

Man must consider and believe with a perfect faith that the Shechina is with him and guards him and protects him. He sees the Creator, and the Creator sees him.

From this, the Hasidim draw the conclusion that the true believer must always, in his contemplation, seek to raise the material things, the "holy sparks" that are in them, to their Divine root, to see the Creator through His garment, and then he will begin to understand everything that happened in the world quite differently. If a man will consider that all the things that attract him or fill him with dread are only transient appearances in a world that was created by one word of the Creator, then he will understand how trivial all his lusts and desires and passions and all his cares and anxieties and fears are, compared with what he has comprehended by the union of his thought with the upper world.

Man, therefore, must not fear anything. "If a man sees any thing of which he is afraid," say the Hasidim, "let him say: 'What is there in this that I need to fear? He (the enemy) is a man like me. So there is nothing to fear. Especially if it is an animal or a beast. It is only that the Holy One has clothed Himself in this thing. Why then should I fear Him?'"

With regard to lust, the Hasidim say:

"If a man sees a beautiful woman let him consider—how did she obtain her beauty? It has come to her from the Divine Power which is spread over her. It is that which bestows on her the gift of beauty. Therefore the source of beauty is Divine Power. Why then should a man be drawn by a part when he would do better to establish his union with the Source?"

The important thing in the way of life of the Hasidim and their conduct is to get rid of grief and sadness. Sorrow and care lead a man to lowness of spirit, when the worship of God requires exaltation of spirit, requires joy. The teaching of Hasidism is: "A man must avoid sorrow as much as he can. Weeping is bad, because a man must serve God with gladness. It is only when the tears are tears of joy that it is good."

God, Man and World

THE WORLD was created, the All out of nothing, out of nihil.

How did nothing become something? This question cannot, according to the Hasidic system of thought, be answered in any way at all, when we consider the *Ayin*, the Infinite Void, as a substance of All—the physical as well as the world of ideas, as a substance of Infinite Void.

For what is the All? The All may be imaginary, an illusion. What man comprehends through his senses is perhaps only his own conception, not the reality. The importance of the All lies in the Divine Infinite Void.

If so, if the All exists only in the human imagination, how did it become a distinct separate thing, an entity? Why does man present it as something in itself? How does man conceive the world as going its own independent way, without feeling the Divine Power that flows and streams through it? More bluntly—how did the idea of the All come to form in the mind of man? Where did he derive the possibility of conceiving the world as though it were divided from the Creator? How did this error develop in man?

The Kabbalists explained it in this way: *Tzimtzum*, Contraction. The Ari, on whose Kabbala Hasidism is based, explains it as follows:

When God consented to create the world there was no empty place in which to establish it, for the Divine Light spread limitlessly (En Sof). Then God contracted the Light, in the way that a garment shrinks when it becomes wet, and He took out the shrunken Light and put it aside. In this way, He cleared an empty space where to establish the world.

Yet even this does not answer the question. As God is All and Everywhere, there is no place free from Him. Then how can we imagine anything that is void and emptied of Him?

Moreover: Even if we assume that an empty space was created, how did it maintain itself? Since there is no place free from God, it could maintain itself only by the power of God. Therefore, the question still remains unanswered. As God is All and Everywhere, and there is nothing where He is not, the All is, in reality His *Ayin*, His Infinite Void. Then everything is not a thing in itself, but a part of *Ayin*. If so, why does man imagine the All as a separate thing? Why does man regard the world as though it were divided and separate from the Creator? How did this universal error originate?

The Hasidim explain it with *Tzimtzum*, Contraction. The Contraction is not, they say, of the Creator, but of the Creation. It is not a reality, but was created in the mind of man.*

God decided to create various things, all that fills the universe, to reveal His Light to every creature. Every creature was created in a limited form, according to the power

---

*Gershon G. Sholem writes of *Tzimtzum* that it is "one of the most amazing and far reaching conceptions ever put forward in the whole history of Kabbalism. *Tzimtzum* originally means 'concentration' or 'contraction,' but if used in Kabbalistic parlance it is best translated by 'withdrawal' or 'retreat'. To the Kabbalists of Luria's (Ari's) school, *Tzimtzum* does not mean the concentration of God at a point, but his retreat away from a point....It means briefly that the existence of the universe is made possible by a process of shrinkage in God." (*Major Trends in Jewish Mysticism*, Rev. ed.—New York: Schocken Books, 1940, p. 260f.)

of conception of each separate kind. Therefore it is impossible for each separate creature to comprehend the fullness of the whole Creation.

It could, for instance, be compared to a teacher trying to explain a difficult matter to a pupil whose mind is not able to grasp it fully. What does the teacher do? He reduces the matter to an elementary stage to fit the mental capacity of the pupil. Does that minimize the matter itself? No! The matter remains as it was. It is reduced, *Tzimtzum*, only in relation to the pupil. It has been brought down from its height to the lower level.

It is also explained in relation to the original thought and its expression. The thought is indeed lofty, but when it has to be explained to others, it can't be transmitted directly—it must be passed on through voice and words which reduce the thought. This creates a situation where those who receive the thought do so in their own way, according to their own capacity, and not infrequently the essential thought dwindles, and may even be completely lost. It is the same with the world. When the creature considers the world, he sees only its exterior, the outer garment, and one who does not look deeper continues under the illusion that he has seen everything.

For the *Tzimtzum* exists only in the imagination, the illusion of the essential All, and through this illusion, man infers that the All is an entity in itself, separate from God.

There is the further complication that the human mind is incapable of comprehending the world fully as a whole, with all its parts together. Man sees only the separate parts, severed from each other, from the greatest part to the smallest, the most minute, each as a thing by itself, a substance, a quality, something independent and self-contained, whole in its own small fragment of the world.

That brings us to the question—how did the world come to be so fragmented, divided into so many small parts? The

Hasidic answer is—*Broken Vessels.*

This conception, which is taken from Kabbala, has a special connotation in Hasidism.

Kabbala explains it thus: The vessels, meaning the whole of Creation, could not bear the intense Light from the Divine that streamed over them ceaselessly. So they broke.

But Hasidism has a profounder explanation. It offers the following interpretation:

What is the deepest, innermost desire of every separate substance, animate or inanimate? It is the desire to exist and never cease to exist. But what is the essential quality of this desire to exist? For eternal existence is included in the nature of every substance. Everything is eternal. Nothing of itself ceases to exist. It ceases to exist only when it has been destroyed by another thing. The desire to exist comes to an entity through the power of inertia established in it, the power of permanence. It is because an entity is a Positive, because it is filled throughout with Existence, with Reality with Being, that it dreads ceasing to be.

That creates the desire to express its own self, its I, the sense of Being. That is the desire of every entity that exists.

In respect to man, it is in the mystery of being human, the expression of his individuality, the sense of his own dignity. And then Hasidism proceeds to explain the Broken Vessels:

As ordinary people consider individualism and separate existence a good thing, creating multiformity a natural blessing, so Hasidism regards it as a great defect.

True beauty, loftiness, blessing and happiness are found only in the Source, in God, in the "Kingdom," in the True Something, not in the something of human experience. But what does man do? He forgets the Source, begins to enjoy the things of his own experience, proclaims himself individualistically and thinks of himself as though he were, himself, the master, the ruler.

That is the meaning of Broken Vessels, that each imagines himself the sole ruler, himself alone, the Kingdom.

But the quality of the Kingdom, of ruler, is bestowed according to Hasidism, only on such an entity that is complete and perfect in itself, and does not need anyone or anything to make it complete and perfect.

Only God is complete and perfect in Himself and none other. Every other being draws its existence from the one and only Source there is, and that is God, the quality of Kingdom, of Ruler.

But when God's creature, man, deludes himself, into imagining that he is himself "Kingdom", Ruler, Monarch, and he does not remember the Source from which he derives his existence, the result is *Broken Vessels*.*

Hasidism has given a lot of thought to the matter of *Tzimtzum*. God did not diminish His Light, but revealed it ac-

---

*Martin Buber explains *Tzimtzum* and *Broken Vessels*, the basic content of the Kabbalistic view which was decisive for Hasidism, that "God contracted himself to world because He, nondual and relationless unity, wanted to allow relation to emerge; because he wanted to be known, loved, wanted; because He wanted to allow to arise from his primally one Being, in which thinking and thought are one, the otherness that strives to unity. So there radiated from Him, the spheres: Separation, creation, formation, making the world of ideas, the forces, the forms, the material, the kingdom of genius, of spirit, of soul, of life; so there was established in them the All, whose 'place' God is and whose center He is.

"...But why was the primal will not satisfied by the pure spheres of separation, the world of ideas, where He who willed to be known could be known face to face? Why must the act bring forth beyond itself ever 'lower,' more distant, shell-enclosed spheres, down to this obdurate, troubled, burdened world in which we creatures, we things live? Why could we not have remained ethereal genius, why had we one after the other to be soiled and permeated with fiery spirit, watery soul, earthly corporeal life?

"To all such questions the Kabbala answers only: God contracted Himself to world. And it is answered, God wanted to be known,

cording to the receptivity of His Creation, the world. There was no restriction, no diminution, only a separate revelation of God.

The Hasidim explain very simply the verse "The whole earth is full of His Glory," as "The Glory of God is everywhere." He fills everything. All that we can see and hear, comprehend and feel, think and observe, all is God.

And one thing follows the other. If the separation of Light is no more than our own idea and not a reality, and God is in fact unlimited, then God fills the lower places of the cosmos no less than the highest; then everything is to Him the same— heaven and earth, past and future, pre-Creation and post-Creation. He was in Tohu-Bohu and he is now in Time and Space. "The Creator fills the whole universe, and there is no place that is void of Him," is the teaching of Hasidism. When one looks at the world, one looks at God, one speaks to the soul that is within one." And

---

loved, wanted, that is: God willed a freely existing, in freedom knowing, in freedom loving, in freedom willing otherness; *he set it free*. This is the concept of *Tsimtsum*, contraction. But while this power, taken away from the Eternal Being, was accorded its freedom, the limitation of its freedom was set by nothing other than its own consequences; it flooded forth beyond its God-near purity." Becoming" broke forth out of "being" what the Kabbala calls 'the mystery of the Breaking of the Vessels' took place. Sphere extended itself out of sphere, world climbed away over world, shell joined itself to shell, unto the limit of the transformations. Here, in the realm of matter that is extended in space, that endures in time, on the rim of what has become, in the uttermost borderland of sense things, God's wave break. The wave that breaks here is God's. As the light from the highest plunged into the lower spheres and shattered them, light-sparks from the primordial being in the immediate presence of God—the genius-natured Adam Kadmon—have fallen into the imprisonment of the things. God's Shekina descends from sphere to sphere, wanders from world to world, banishes itself in shell after shell until it reaches its furthest exile: us. In our world God's fate fulfilled. But our world is in truth the world of man." (*The Origin and Meaning of Hasidism*—New York: Horizon Press, 1960, pp. 118-121.)

the soul is surely a spark of God.

All that a man sees, he sees as no disconnected Positive, but as the Life of God that proceeds from it. Every substance is Divine and what is changed is only the form. The moral of this is that man does not have to seek God in secret places. He can find God in everything that surrounds him, and, of course, he can find Him also in himself. God, who is hidden in the secrecy of His Power, sends His Word to man, calls to him aloud, speaks to his heart: "Behold me! I am near, I am very near to you!"

All things that are in this material world, and all the qualities contained in them are no more than a parable from which we must draw the moral; and only this, the moral, is the sense and the meaning of the Divine quality that it contains. Each thing contains a hint, an indication, a suggestion of the Divine—in each movement, in every motion, in every whisper, in every murmur, in everything, in all that we feel and see and hear.

"When you go out," Hasidism teaches, "and you hear people talk, penetrate into the words, into what they contain, join them one to another, purify them from their ordinary week-day dross, remove their coarse outer cover, lift them to their spiritual essence, to what is permanent, to what is eternal—and you will see in them the Divine."

And when one looks deeply and one sees the mystery of nature and its laws, one sees the loftiness of the Divine. Look up to the sky and count the stars! Man can see God's majesty and wonder especially when he watches the stars in their courses, how they shed light, and from this he can attain to the understanding of how to appreciate God's greatness.

How do Hasidim explain the evil, the wickedness in man, if God is in everything and in all, and naturally, therefore, most of all in man? Is God also evil?

Hasidim answer: When you see bad, depraved conduct,

ugly passions, lusts, look into their inner nature, look to the essential joy and power which is in them, and you will see that they are nothing else than the Exile of the Shechina—the Shechina which God divided off from Himself to accompany the People of Israel in their Exile, into which they were banished because of the sins they had committed.

When a man suddenly feels a flow of fine and lofty thoughts, emotions that are pure and clean, too fine to be discerned by the heart, and man's gaze is sharpened till the contours appear of all the generations and of all the deeds that are done, God calls to him, and man feels with his whole being that all and everything has a deep meaning, that all he sees every day, that appears to him accidental, chance, without significance, of little consequence, has quite a different aspect—it is the revelation of what is veiled in secret mystery; and man feels that not the slightest blade of grass, not the tiniest creature, but is an indication of higher worlds.

GOD REVEALS Himself to man through these five further ways:

A) Through thoughts of penitence which come to a man each day. Man is sunk in lust, in cares, anxieties, and suddenly he thinks about his life that he squanders in trivialities, thinks about the sins he commits against his own spirit, about the vanities with which he occupies himself, about the Divine from which he has turned aside, and to which he now wishes to return.

B) Through the fear that suddenly assails a man. He sits hidden from everything and all, doing ugly things, thinking evil thoughts, then suddenly he steps back shaken, trembling, as though a sword had smitten him. What has he seen? He has seen what one sees who gazes into the depths of his heart.

C) Through the vision of the permanence and eternity of nature, the eternal wisdom, the heavenly expanse, the infinity of space.

D) Through the sense of bliss existing in every one of God's creatures, the love placed in it through the Act of Creation.

E) Through the marvellous grace that is put into each created thing, through the loveliness of each creature, through the mystery of the Shechina that rests on every thing—from a blade of grass to a tree, from the smallest bird to an eagle, from the tiniest animal to an elephant—and to the Crown of Creation, Man.

But most of all, God reveals Himself in the Torah. The Torah is the absolute essential substance of God transmitted in human speech, in human history, human laws and regulations. The Torah is Divine not only as a complete whole, but each letter is a special Divine Revelation, and the composition of its letters is the composition of letters through which the world was created.

When a man occupies himself with the Torah, he is not only fulfilling the precept to learn and study Torah, but he is wrapped up and absorbed in the substance of the Divine. The Divine surrounds him on all sides, it has penetrated into him and through him, for "The Torah and Holiness, Bless His Name, are One."

The Jewish faith assumes that the Torah was given from Heaven. Hasidim say that too, but they add that the Torah is the essence of Heaven—it is not only Divine, it is the Divinity itself. And as, according to Hasidism, the expression of God is the expression of the world, and the expression of the world is the expression of God, so also the sense and meaning of the Torah is the sense and meaning of the world, and the sense and meaning of the world is the sense and meaning of the Torah. Not only is "Israel and the Torah a Unity," but so is "The World and the Torah a Unity." And in both the world and the Torah, we can reveal God, see the hidden mystery that is concealed in them. The Torah is eternal not only because God gave it for eternity, but because it is the essence of Holiness. No one can exhaust the Torah, because the Torah is endless and inexhaustible.

THERE IS a firm belief in Hasidism that man is capable of recognizing the holiness and the exalted beauty there is in every thing, of comprehending the absolute unity that exists even in division, in severance, in contradictions, in dismemberment, in what appears to be the error of Being. In viewing the world, Hasidim see the Lord of the world. They destroy the barriers, they tear down the veils that hold apart God and the world. They say that when man perceives and recognizes all these things, when he dwells in holiness, then all he sees, hears, and encounters on his way leads straight to the source—to the Will of God. All the things he uses, all that gives him pleasure, everything he eats and drinks, all that he uses to dress himself and adorn himself—every single object, every individual thing with which he has any contact—it all divests itself of its every-day garb and robes itself in holiness, ascends from the deepest depths and rises to the heights, casts off vulgarity and defilement, and shines with the radiance of the Shechina.

Man should perceive the specific light there is in every creature, their particular bright manifestations, their qualities that lift them to high levels, the special intentions inherent in every thing, in every happening. And when man thinks deeply about everything he sees, about every encounter, conception, idea and act, and lives with the right intentions, he gradually raises the degraded, cleanses the polluted, clarifies the nebulous, purifies the vulgarized and the gross.

But if, on the contrary, man has not in mind the Source from which he comes, sinks into himself, regards himself as the center, he is not a redeemer in the world; he does harm to the world—not only does he not save the holy sparks that have sunk deep into the depths, but he makes new sparks from the bright heavens to sink into the deep impure depths.

Man has a sublime soul, an understanding of purity, a yearning for holiness. But woe to the man who instead of elevating his natural beauty to the high level of sublimated beauty, plunges into sensuality, sinks into physical lust, tears off the royal robe from his soul, and flings away the shreds into the dung heap. Man must be like the bee that converts the juices of flowers into honey. Woe to him who does the contrary.

THESE ARE grave matters with which Hasidism engages itself, and they cannot be spoken about in a light and popular manner. But in spite of this, Hasidism stands face to face with the folk; the simple folk, too, wish to penetrate the mysteries of being and not being, of Positive and Negative, of *Yesh* and *Ayin*.

And the folk ask other grave questions as well. How does one explain them all to the folk? One can't speak to ordinary people with the language of Ibn Gabbai, Moses Cordovero or the Holy Ari. The ordinary folk won't understand it.

The founder of Hasidism, Rabbi Israel Baal Shem Tov, found the answer.

RABBI ISRAEL BAAL SHEM TOV

ISRAEL, THE future Baal Shem Tov, known by his initials as Besht, was as a child left an orphan, having lost both parents, and when kind people sent him to cheder he ran away. They found him wandering in the forest, enraptured by nature. The people who were looking after him gave him up as "wild and undisciplined." They said they couldn't do a thing with him. So he grew up without control or supervision. He became an assistant to a melamed, taking the children to cheder and synagogue, teaching them simple prayers, the benedictions, the sanctification. When he took the children to synagogue, he led them, singing aloud, and they sang with him, and his song was sweet and pleasant.

Picture it—a small boy, poor, of no particular family, heading a big band of children through the streets singing a hymn from the liturgy, and all the children singing with him, and the people of the town stand watching, listening wondering, feeling a sense of contrition and of repentance.

So as to understand the origin of Hasidism, the seed from which it grew, we must consider this—a small, lonely orphan boy runs away from cheder and wanders alone through the forest; and this same boy, when he is put in charge of other children (probably not much younger than himself), leads them through the streets, singing with them with such sweetness that the people of the town are astonished. And this boy later becomes the Baal Shem Tov, the founder of Hasidism.

The legend goes on to tell us that the voice of this little orphan boy split the heavens, and gave those in the heights a special pleasure, like that with which people used to listen of old to the sweet singing of the Levites in the Temple.

At 13, Israel became a Shamash, a caretaker-sacristan in a synagogue. There he had the opportunity of getting to know the rabbinical learned atmosphere of the Beth Hamedrash. He listened to the quibbling arguments of the scholars, and they did not capture his heart. He already felt, says the legend, that this was not the way. It was dry-as-dust, it lacked warmth, it lacked the juice of the soul of Jewishness. It was not the clear soul-refreshing sweetness of Jewishness that he felt in his heart.

So he left the synagogue and did various kinds of work

—all sorts of things—to earn his bread. He wandered through the streets of the town, but he found no peace for his soul.

He left the town and the people. And far from the walls of the synagogue, far from the noise and the murmur of the studies of the rabbis and the scholars at their learned disputations, he wandered through fields and forests, among mountains and valleys. Under the blue skies, in the wide open spaces, God's Glory was revealed to him, the Glory of the God of the great expanses, the God of the Prophets and the Kabbalists, the God of Israel.

For seven years he lived in seclusion, given up to contemplation, mediating on the foundation of the world, and its relation to the people of Israel, the wisdom of Israel, the soul of Israel. And when he had realized the meaning of it all, the time came for him to be revealed to the world. As though a Voice from Heaven had spoken to him: "Arise and return to your brethren, go back to your people, and be a leader to them, show them the roads that lead to God! Arise! The time has come!"

And when he came back to the people and saw how foolish and confused their way of life was, how the rabbis and scholars and communal leaders misinterpreted everything, and the shuls were cold and musty, his heart sank: "Woe!" he cried. "The world is so full of wonders that gladden the heart and bring light to the eyes, and here there is blindness all round!"

Then he began to preach how to recognize God; he began to open the eyes of the people who were blind. And many left their benches in the Beth Hamedrash, shut their Gemaras, stopped cudgelling their heads with argument and disputation, and followed him, to hear Torah from his lips.

Even some renowned rabbis, whose Jewishness had previously consisted of study and fasting, laws and regulations, became his followers, and adopted his way of life and conduct.

Many Kabbalists, too, listened to what the young Baal Shem Tov preached and accepted his Torah.

But, as already pointed out, the Baal Shem Tov's Torah of Hasidism was not essentially anything new. It was the same old Jewish Torah, newly adjusted to life—the same Torah of the Prophets and the sages, of Halacha and Aggada, and above all Kabbala, the Torah of plain and simple belief in God, with man rising towards the Divine in the way of Kabbala, and man's close approach to God. It was intimacy after the fashion of the common folk, a Torah without profound, intricate rabbinical hair-splitting—the Torah of ecstasy and of complete surrender of self to God, the Torah of love and compassion that comes from the depths of the heart.

Reb Israel Baal Shem Tov went about in the towns and villages, through streets and market places, preaching the lofty ideas and the holy words of the Kabbalists which till then had been known only to a select few. He now brought them to the masses of the people. He told them in the simple language of the people, adapting them to the mind and spirit of the ordinary common man. He clothed his thoughts in fables and allegories and stories taken from their ordinary everyday life. He appeared in a market place and spoke to the stall-holders and the shopkeepers, busy with their business, having no thought of God and Judaism. He stopped a few Jews and talked to them about some ordinary matter, and gradually led the conversation towards God and His wonders, about man and the nature of man, and the relationship between God and man. He spoke simply, so that all could understand. Soon a small crowd gathered round him: "The Baal Shem is here!" And he stood in the middle of the crowd and preached to them, repeating his words, explaining God and His ways to them in the language and with the example of familiar things—about a horse and a calf, about corn and about merchandise.

"In every thing there are worlds. Everywhere there is soul, spirit, Godliness." He comforted them: "God wants us to serve Him in all manner of ways; we can find union with Him in every way. Both through the words of the Torah, through learned study, through prayer, through ordinary simple talk with a man in the market place."

And these ordinary people went home, spiritually elevated—they, the poor shopkeepers and market traders and artisans, overlooked by all, pushed aside, were not lost. So the Baal Shem Tov had assured them.

Israel Baal Shem Tov, the Besht, was not a writer. His Torah was written down by others, not by him. He himself had no great regard for the written word, the dead letters, the book. As one sifts much sand to discover a tiny diamond, so he sifted through the pages of many books to discover a hidden thought which he could clothe with flesh and skin and set in the midst of life, to bring it to the people and enrich its spirit, give it meaning and understanding.

And the people believed the Besht, listened to him. They venerated him as a saint, a Zaddik. They followed him. Legends grew up around him; marvellous tales were told about him. They passed from mouth to mouth, and travelled like a song over great distances—"A redeemer has come to us Jews!"

There are people who always want to establish the exact facts, and who find inconsistencies and contradictions in the Besht's Torah. But they cannot diminish, they cannot mar his Torah. Who of the great spiritual leaders of mankind is without contradictions? Not the Prophets. Even the Bible itself has passages that contradict each other.

The Besht's Torah has no definite line or order. Like the Prophets, the Besht was no logician, no thinker. "They speak the words that God puts into their mouth," the Prophets said of themselves. That is also true of the Besht.

His thoughts were rays of light, sparks of fire from God's flame. He did not quote from learned books. He didn't like repeating someone else's thoughts. His words came from his own heart and mind, not from texts. He sought God not in books, nor in the Messorah, but from round himself—from nature, from life, among the mass of the people, in the market, in everyday talk, in a simple tune. "Even a Gentile tune contains a Divine spark," he said. God was to him a direct inner revelation. He saw God in everything, in the whole of life. "If you avoid life," he taught, "you avoid God. One reaches God only through life, through eating and drinking, through joy and pleasure. For everything is the Living God. And if you suppress and kill the life, the desire, the longing which are also part of God, you kill God Himself."

Moreover the Besht preached: "Not like one humiliated and despised, not like a slave before his master are you to live in the created world, in the world that is Divine, but proudly and happily."

And the Besht told men: "Even if one stumbles and sins, one must not fall into despair." He explained this by saying that one often imagines one has committed a sin, when it is in reality no sin, "but an act of Satan, who wants to drag a man down to sadness and melancholy, which is itself a sin."

Israel Besht was a man who enjoyed life, unlike the Ari and his companions, who turned their backs on life and practiced self-denial. It is not only permissible to live—it is your duty to live. This was Besht's teaching. Life must not be a need, something imposed, but a desire, a striving. But this life, this desire and striving, must be in holiness. Even the material in man must be linked with the intention to achieve union with God and the Shechina. We must conceive of life as God gave it: one with its lust and passion, laughter and enjoyment and pleasure. We must not weaken life, and diminish it, its ways and its habits. Because everything is God. Even in sin there is God. "The Shechina is even in sexual intercourse."

We must live and sweeten the evil, said the Besht, for there is no such thing as absolute evil. "Evil is a pedestal for the good," he said. "Even falsehood contains a spark of Truth." We must enjoy life, but we must do so in a pure and holy manner. Enjoy life, but at the same time seek union with God.

This is what the Besht taught the people, who were used to hearing that they must renounce pleasure, who were always being admonished and castigated and threatened with terrible punishment awaiting those who did not carefully observe the commandments. These people had been told the story of the Ari who had once seen a man long dead, because once on a Sabbath he had unwittingly carried a little sand out of doors in his shoes. To these people the Besht preached a living God, to whom they could come, not through fasting and self-mortification, but through the joy of life, through the mystic concealment that is in one's heart.

THIS IS the Besht, and this is the essence of his teaching, of his Torah which he brought to the people. It is now more than 200 years since the Besht died, and since his death much has been added in Hasidism to his simplicity, and much has been subtracted. Since his time there have been such interpreters of Hasidism as Rabbi Shneour Zalman of Liady, who transformed the simple Beshtian Hasidism into a recondite philosophy, a new abstruse scholarship that only the select few can understand. There have also been other interpreters of Hasidism, who have given it new meanings. But the essence of Hasidism was and has remained what the Besht brought to the people at the beginning: religious enthusiasm, ecstasy, a spark of God's flame that penetrates the heart of man and blazes up with a holy fire.

The Besht's Hasidism is pure Jewish mysticism, Jewish

Kabbala, whose beginnings we find in the Bible, and whose further development was expressed by the author or authors of the Zohar and the later Kabbalists, especially those of Safad and their interpreters in Poland and other places.

RABBI NACHMAN BRATZLAVER

There is a mountain and on that mountain is
    a stone,
From that stone runs a spring,
And each thing has a heart,
And the world as a whole has a heart.

And the heart is opposite the spring.
And it longs and yearns always to reach the spring,
And the longing and yearning of the heart for the
    spring is wild,
And it is always crying out because it wants to
    reach the spring,
And the spring craves for the heart,
And the longing of both for each other is more than
    can be borne

If the heart would not see the spring,
It would die, God forbid, of longing,
For all its life is from the spring.
And if the heart died, God forbid, of longing,
The whole world would die.

Because the heart is the life of every living thing,
Of the whole world—
And how can the world exist without the heart.

And the spring has no time,
For it has no day and no time in the world at all—

For it is above the time of the world,
And the time of the spring is only when the heart
    gives it a day as a gift,
And when the day is about to end,
They begin to bid each other farewell,
The heart and the spring,
And they tell each other parables and sing songs
    to each other,
With great love and great longing.

And the true man of grace and good deeds
Comes and gives the heart a day,
And the heart gives the day to the spring.
And so the spring again has a day.

And when the day comes it also comes with
    parables and with songs
In which all the wisdoms are.
And there are differences between the days,
For there are Sundays and Mondays and so on,
And new moons and festivals.
And each day comes with its own songs,
According to the day.

CAN THESE lines be described as poetry? To answer this question we must first decide, what is poetry? Webster defines poetry as "language chosen and arranged to create a specific emotional response, a quality that stirs the imagination." According to this definition the lines are poetry. They certainly "stir the imagination."

Is there mysticism in the lines? Definitely! It is the song of a mystic. One who does not see the world in a mystic light can't make head or tail of such ideas. And one who is not a poet can't give expression to such ideas, to such metaphors. And the remarkable thing about it is that the poet-mystic who wrote these lines didn't know he was a poet, that he was creating works of art. Of course, he didn't describe himself as a poet-mystic, one who visualizes spiritual treasures, converts dreams into reality, is a seer, in the sense of his soul desiring all the beautiful and exalted things that shine in the wide stretches of the world, and which are seen more clearly and more deeply, according to the seer's power of vision.

It is even more remarkable that this poet-mystic never wrote down his works, neither poetry nor prose. They were written down by someone else, one of his followers, one of his disciples, one of his devoted Hasidim. He himself, this poet-mystic, like one of the troubadours, a bard, a folk-singer, of old, improvised his verses, his ballads, his stories, his fables, his parables, his allegories; he told them or declaimed them to his hearers, not knowing even what declaiming was. He called his works simply stories, and without realizing what he was doing left a rich legacy for many generations.

This poet-mystic was Rabbi Nachman Bratzlaver, Rabbi Nachman of Bratzlav. He was born in 1772, and died in 1810, at the early age of 38. He was a great-grandson of the Besht, Israel Baal Shem Tov, the founder of Hasidism.

He was one of those exceptional spiritual figures whose fate it is to be engaged in a constant, ceaseless struggle with himself, with the tragic contradictions in life, whose only accompaniment on their sad road is grief, garbed in the black robe of loneliness.

Loneliness—for while he felt the sadness in the great mystery of the road of life, those who were his Hasidim looked up to him as one to whom everything was revealed, one who saw in everything a hidden great joy, and was able to reveal that joy also to them. But he himself knew no joy. He saw more mystery than revelation in the sense of his own being, and what was for himself a mystery he could not reveal to others.

So he took to speaking in hints and suggestions, and the hint was his poetic expression, which his Hasidim accepted as holiness, as the symbol of the deep meaning of the Infinite. Rabbi Nachman was a great man with a unique approach, which was original, not accepted tradition. He brought with him something different, which rouses suspicion and anger among those who are afraid to leave the trodden roads. His teachings, his stories, his whole conduct was not understood. Some Hasidim opposed him fiercely; they even suspected him of heresy—others said he was out of his mind. The Hasidic world didn't understand him and persecuted him, because he did not go in their ways. They warned against him. As often happens with people of great spirit Rabbi Nachman was a riddle to the men of his time. But he, we are told, said that his light would not go out till Messiah would come. And so it seems to be. His light today is bright and it grows brighter the more he is recognized.

NATURE endowed Nachman richly from his birth. He, the Besht's great-grandson, was born with a great and far-reaching imagination, with a spark of original poetry, a restless spirit that searched and probed endlessly for what was hidden and concealed, a tender feeling heart that bore in itself the griefs of the world, the sufferings of whole generations. And this child grew up in the mystical surrounding of Hasidism, where the whole atmosphere was soaked with miracles and wonders, and the most amazing stories about the Baal Shem Tov and his Hasidim. Nachman listened to those stories with bated breath; they carved themselves into his mind.

When he was six, Nachman was already walking in the fear of Heaven, fasting, without his mother knowing. He pretended to be eating the food she prepared for him, but in reality he fasted. On the eve of each Sabbath he went to the *Mikvah*, and then in his Sabbath clothes hurried to the *Beth*

Hamedrash, and with childish steps paced impatiently up and down, waiting for the Sabbath sanctity to make itself felt, for his soul to quiver. Once—so he afterwards related to his Hasidim—he was only six—he had hugged a stand in the synagogue and trembling had listened to one of the great Hasidim singing with ecstasy the *Song of Songs,* and gradually his singing became a sobbing and weeping. And he too, the six-year old, poured out his heart to God in prayer and tears.

Often of an evening little Nachman ran to the grave of his great-grandfather, the Besht, to plead with him to explain to him the nature of God. He knew the text, "I see God always against me," and he tried with closed eyes to depict to himself the image of God. He wasn't content with the set forms of the prayers in the *Siddur.* He liked to go to a remote corner and talk things over with God, in ordinary everyday Yiddish speech, the Yiddish of his mother's Yiddish prayer book.

According to the custom of those days young Nachman was married off at 13. He moved to the village of Husyatin, where his rich father-in-law lived. He loved the countryside, the rural scene. It impressed itself on his poetic-mystic soul. He had a small boat in which he used to row out to some distant quiet corner, and stay there for hours. He was a horseman. He would ride deep into the forest, let the horse wander, and he poured out his heart in prayer to God —not the ready-made prayers of the *Siddur,* but his own improvisations in Yiddish, in the mother-tongue.

Later, when he was already the famous Rabbi, he used to say to his Hasidim that when you say your prayers in the open, the grasses all round enter into your prayer, and help you and strengthen you in your prayer. Then each word is a whole world; while the man prays it is as though he were picking flowers and weaving them into a garland.

By the time he was 26 Rabbi Nachman was already

accepted as a Zaddik, and he had his own circle of Hasidim. Then he decided to do what his great-grandfather the Baal Shem Tov wanted to do and had not been able to accomplish—to make what was at that time the long and hazardous journey to Palestine, to the Land of Israel. It took him more than a year, that journey, round which his Hasidim afterwards wove a crown of tales and legends. The Land of the Patriarchs impressed the young mystic tremendously. "All the life I have," he used to say later, "comes only from my having been in *Eretz Israel*. When he returned from the journey Rabbi Nachman settle in Bratzlav; he spent his most fruitful years there.

Bratzlav became an integral part of him—he has gone down in Jewish history as Nachman Bratzlaver, Rabbi Nachman of Bratzlav. He found his most devoted Hasidim in Bratzlav. It was there he met Nathan Nemirover, the man whose name is inextricably linked with his own, Nathan Nemirover, who simply worshiped Rabbi Nachman. Nathan Nemirover was a scholar and a man with the gift of words. He became Rabbi Nachman's scribe, his amanuensis. He wrote down the Rabbi's sermons, and everything he said his conversations, his table talk. For he was convinced that in every word that came from Rabbi Nachman's lips three were concealed deep mysteries. Thanks to Nathan of Nemirov, we have had preserved for us all that Rabbi Nachman taught, the treasures of his wonderful mind and soul, and his poetic works, his fables and parables, the tales that he told. Nathan of Nemirov went to great pains to see that the Rabbi's literary legacy should be preserved. He had the works printed and published after Rabbi Nachman's death.

Yet it is not easy to get to know Rabbi Nachman's world of ideas. Because he was all his short life engaged in a constant conflict, a conflict between the poet and the mystic. It resulted in a series of tragic contradictions. We must remember that this true saint, gifted with such a rich imagi-

nation, a real poet, with a keen and searching spirit, grew
up in an environment of mysticism, trained in Kabbala-liter-
ature, where ideas and astonishing poetic images were cou-
pled with all sorts of symbols and plays on words. We therefore often find in Rabbi Nachman brilliant flashes of
thought, inspired ideas and deep emotion that must be dug
out from under a heap of sand and rubble.

According to Rabbi Nachman the most beautiful thing in
the world is melody. Melody—he says—is like the three
prime colors of the rainbow; melody is the robe of the
Shechina. One must have a knowledge of music in order to
understand how to collect everywhere all the scattered
melodies and construct out of them compositions, create the
joy, the spirit of prophecy, which is the absolute contrary of
sadness. For only when the Prophet grasps the melody
through which the musician creates the absolute joy can the
spirit of prophecy awaken in him.

"He often," Nathan Nemirover tells us of Rabbi Nachman Bratzlaver, "he often sang one of his own melodies, one
of his own compositions, and singing it he began to dance;
and one who has not seen him dance has in his whole life
seen nothing so good."

Rabbi Nachman Bratzlaver who always carried in his
heart the grief of the world, was himself full of sadness—his
soul was always engaged in a struggle between poetic skepticism and mystic faith—always preached to his followers:
"We must be always joyful and serve God with joy."
"Another dance!" he used to say to his Hasidim. "We must
remove from us sorrow, must be always mindful to be in a
happy mood."

He himself, Rabbi Nachman Bratzlaver, the ascetic, who
as a child afflicted his body and kept constant fasts, never
stopped warning his followers to have compassion on their
own bodies, to purify their bodies, so that the soul should be
able to transmit to it the conceptions to which it has attained.

"The wicked," said the Bratzlaver, "sing mostly melodies of grief and lamentations. One can recognize by a man's melodies the road he is going—the roads of wickedness or the roads of righteousness." "You should know," he told his followers, "that each spot has its own separate melody. Each blade of grass has its song, and through the grasses that grow out of the ground and thrive there the melody is created. That is why each herdsman, each shepherd has his own special melody, according to the grasses that grow there while he is feeding his cattle or his sheep. Thanks to the melody the spirit of man rises above all the creatures of the earth; the melody liberates man from the spirit of the beast, lifts his spirit to the heights, while the spirit of the beast remains stuck below."

Rabbi Nachman was once walking in a field with one of his Hasidim, and he said to him: "If you had the privilege of hearing the songs of praise of the grasses and vegetation! Each blade of grass sings the praise of the Creator, without any other intent, without ulterior motives, without any thought of reward. How fine and lovely it is when we hear this song of the grass! It is good to be devout in their company! How delightful it is to go out in the field in the early spring, when nature is awakening from her sleep, and there to pour out your prayer to God! Each fresh blade of grass that grows, each flower—they all merge into one melody; for they too long and yearn for God."

"There are fields," the Bratzlaver exclaims, "and trees grow there and plants, vegetation saturated with beauty, and the glory of these blossoming fields is impossible to describe! Happy is the eye that can see it! For all these trees and all this vegetation—they are like holy souls that grow and thrive there. And there are still so many naked souls that wander about lost, from the other side of the border of these blossoming fields, waiting for redemption."

The mystic Rabbi Nachman saw the whole cosmos woven together in one knot. "You must know," he said to his Hasidim, "the world is like a top. Always spinning. Everything is in constant motion, and endlessly changing its form. A man becomes an angel; an angel becomes a man. Everything is in constant motion and change. One is transformed into another, a constant ascent from the lower and a descent from the height. For everything stems from one root, and it is all a complete unity."

"God," he said another time, "does not create the same thing twice, for everything keeps changing its form."

He himself, the Bratzlaver, was also in constant motion; he was the tireless seeker. "I can't," he said, "stand still on the same level. It is not good to be old. We must keep always renewing ourselves, for it is only through constant renewal, through endless striving that we have revealed to us the most sublime, the loveliest thing in the world, the melody. You should know that each wisdom in the world has its separate song and melody that belongs to it alone."

He certainly had his own song and melody that belonged to him alone and that marked him out not only as the great mystic and saint, but and essentially so as the great poet. In the last years of his brief life he found a garment in which to robe his mysticism, a poetic garment, and he passed it on to his pupils through his tales of fantasy, rich and imaginary— which make the first lovely page in our new Yiddish literature.

"I am going to start telling stories," the Bratzlaver said to his followers. Unfortunately these stories have not come down to us in their original form, for he did not write them himself. He only told them, and his devoted disciple Nathan Nemirover wrote them down afterwards from memory. Nathan Nemirover was a scholar and a man versed in Kabbala, but we can't know how truly he retold his stories, how much of Rabbi Nachman's rich imagery was lost in the retelling.

Thirteen stories were preserved by Nathan Nemirover, who afterwards had them printed. Most of the stories are of a general character. There is only one story which is really Jewish—the story of a Rabbi and his only son. It is a typical Hasidic tale. It is the story of a Rabbi, a *Mithnagid*, a dry as dust scholar, whose acute scholarly wisdom is unable to satisfy his son, who has a sensitive soul. The son is drawn toward the Hasidic Rebbe, the Zaddik of the generation, who alone can refresh his heart. The *Mithnagidic* Rabbi, the father, won't have it. He puts all sorts of obstacles in his son's way. And the poor son longs and yearns; his heart is faint with desire for the Rebbe, the fountain-head of the new life.

There is biting irony in the Bratzlaver' s story of the *Wise Man and the Fool*—a satire through which he brings out his basic idea that to the things that happen in life we must come with ordinary simplicity, that it is foolish of the rationalists to want to take everything apart and explain it with their reason: those who think that everything in the world can be explained with plain common sense.

"Things happen," said the Bratzlaver, "that are the opposite of rational, and man's logic cannot explain them. If man relies only on his reason he may fall into many errors and knock against stumbling-blocks."

He told the story of two friends, one foolish and the other wise, with a lot of accumulated knowledge. The fool goes with sure tread over the crooked ways of life, and the wise man with his continual reasoning and doubting is flung from one disaster to another, and ends up in the deep slough.

It is possible that in ridiculing his wise man who ended up in the slough, Rabbi Nachman meant to make light of the scholarship and wisdom which he himself possessed and for which he was highly reputed. The simple unlearned man, he tells us, who asked no questions and didn't bother his head with involved reasoning, and was always happy though he owned nothing—maybe because he owned nothing—rose in time to wisdom also. Through simple faith and the strength of simple faith he became a great lord, the lord of lords, in the realm of the King; through simplicity he attained wisdom and knowledge. For he who believes simply, the holy simpleton, whom all consider a fool, he has in him the basis of all the wisdom in the world: the trustful, joyful heart. While the wise man on the other hand is at bottom a fool—too much thinking, too much reasoning, leading ultimately to disbelief, to denial of everything he doesn't actually see. With the result that he sinks in the slough.

Here is another tale, a parable about the greed that leads people astray:

A man is wakened at night by someone knocking at his window, and saying: "If you want to buy a fine horse cheap, come out, and I'll show it to you."

The man went out, saw the horse, which was really very fine, asked the price and found it was astonishingly cheap. The horse was worth at least double. He paid the money, and was sure that he could sell it at a big profit. In the morning, he led the horse to the market. Soon a man came along and offered him twice the price he had paid for the horse. But he wouldn't sell. He wanted more. Another man offered him four times as much, but that only convinced him that the horse was worth much more. He decided that only the King could afford to pay him the proper price for such a horse. It was indeed a horse such as one would expect to find only in the King's stables. The King was terribly excited when the horse was brought to him—he had never seen a horse like that anywhere in the world. He offered a mint of money for it. And the man again decided not to sell. Why should he sell a horse for which the King himself offered such a tremendous price? It must be priceless!

He took the horse away from the King's palace. On the

way he stopped, to let it drink. Suddenly the horse was gone! Only the glint of its hoofs could be seen in the distance. The man started shouting: "My horse! The most valuable horse in the world!" People came running up, shook him, tried to calm him. "What horse?" they cried. "There was no horse! You're dreaming. We saw you come here, and you had no horse with you! It was a dream."

But the man did not stop shouting and screaming, until the people got angry, because he was disturbing everybody by making such a row, and they started to hit him, saying that he was a madman, and ought be put in an asylum. In the end the man really went mad.

The moral is not to be greedy. The horse possibly never existed, except in the man's imagination. The whole transaction, his buying the horse at night, when he was awakened from his sleep, suggests that it was only a dream. But it drove him mad.

Sometimes the whole world has gone mad. And it doesn't know that it's mad. Only a few very wise people realize their own madness. There was another story the Bratzlaver told:

The King said one day to his Viceroy: "I see in the stars that the harvest this year will be mad. Those who eat of this year's crop will go mad. What advice have you to give—what shall we eat this year?"

The Viceroy's advice was: "Decree that enough corn of last year's crop should be put aside to last us through the year; and we will not eat of this year's crop."

But the advice did not please the King. "What good will it do us," he asked, "if everybody is mad, and we two alone are sane? The mad people will say that we are the mad ones. Couldn't we find enough corn from last year's crop for everybody?"

"We can't. There isn't enough!"

"Then there is only one way for us," said the King. "We

shall all have to eat of the same mad crop as everybody else. But we'll do something to make us different—we will know that we are mad."

"How," asked the Viceroy, "will we two know that we are mad? Mad people don't know that they are mad."

"We'll put a mark on our foreheads," said the King. "When we look at each other and we see the mark on our foreheads we'll know that we are mad; in that way we will be different."

There is something profound in this story. It is no use being sane in a mad world. Where all are mad the sane man is abnormal. And we know what happens to abnormal people in a mad world. They fill the prisons and the concentration camps. The only way is to put a mark on your forehead, so that you know that you're mad.

RABBI NACHMAN didn't just tell his stories for the sake of telling stories. There was always some reason for it, and some special occasion that moved him to tell his story as an illustration.

Once, for instance, some of his Hasidim were talking about Napoleon's big victories at that time. They were astonished how a man of such low origin could rise so high, to become an Emperor.

"Who knows," said the Bratzlaver, "where his soul comes from? Sometimes souls are interchanged."

And he went on to tell the story of a king's son and the son of a servant, who were changed for each other.

Another time when he heard that Nathan Nemirover had written to another Hasid that he must always be happy, the Bratzlaver said: "I'll tell you how people used to be happy." And he went on to tell the STORY OF THE SEVEN BEGGARS, a real poem, which is the crown of all Rabbi Nachman Bratzlaver's stories. It is one of the profoundest, one of the most beautiful stories in the whole of Yiddish literature. In telling us the story of the beggars Rabbi Nachman reveals to us the whole world of ideas that he had built up through countless experiences and sufferings and doubts.

The poet-mystic is firmly convinced that the road to the sublimest heights lies only through suffering, that the grief of the world and the black night of the world are pierced by the rays of God's Light—we need only have eyes to see.

The demands that everyday life makes on us are petty and of no account. The noise and bustle of the market place is discordant and harsh. Yet one who has a sensitive ear will hear the wonderful melody that sounds through the cosmos, the great joy that springs out of the deep sorrow of the world. It is a tale to be read and re-read and pondered over, with its allusions and symbols. It is a gem not only in Yiddish but in world literature.

"There is a hill," Rabbi Nachman Bratslaver tells us, "and on that hill is a stone. From that stone runs a spring. And each thing has a heart, and the world as a whole has a heart.

"And the heart is opposite the spring, and it longs and yearns always to reach the spring. And the longing and yearning of the heart for the spring is wild."

"Should for any length of time," continues Rabbi Nachman, "the heart lose sight of the spring, it will perish along with the world. For how can the world exist without the heart?"

Let us consider: Who are the heart of the world? They are those in whom the whole life of the world is concentrated. In the way in which the rays of the sun are concentrated in a burning-glass. Those who always move the world and will not let it stay in one place. Those who drive the world on, urging it further and further, lifting it higher and higher. Those who give a meaning to life, a value, a direction.

What is the spring on the mountain? It is what we cannot define with any word, yet we feel it is there, and only there that we must turn, though unconsciously, by instinct, through super-consciousness. This mystical tendency of man is the spring on the mountain.

"And the heart is always crying out," Rabbi Nachman continues, "because it wants to reach the spring. And the spring craves for the heart."

"Then why," the Bratzlaver asks, " if the heart craves so much for the spring, doesn't it go to the spring?" And he sets out the different obstacles that stand in the way, and will not let the heart reach the spring. But it isn't that which is so important. What is important is that "if the heart would not see the spring it would die. And if the heart died, the whole world would die, because the heart is the life of every living thing. And how can the world exist without the heart?"

That is why the heart cannot reach the spring; but it is always opposite the spring, and it longs and yearns for it; and its yearning and longing to reach the spring is wild.

Let us consider the deep meaning, the symbolism of "the heart of the world," and "the spring." The heart of the world must for ever want to reach the spring, long and yearn for it, without being able to reach it. At the same time the heart of the world must for ever see the eternal spring, for "if the heart does not see the spring it would die." It means that man must always have the highest ideal before him, and want to reach it, long for it and yearn and never stop yearning for it. What is this highest ideal? Jewish tradition is very clear about that: The Messianic ideal! If man did not see this fountain, the source, the world would die!

Sometimes the heart of the world is sick and faint. Man does not always see the sense and meaning of the world and of what is done in it. Man is not always clear about where he is to strive for. He goes about perplexed, in doubt, misled. And the far-seeing, clear-thinking, and deep-feeling men see it and cannot help. They lift their eyes despairingly to heaven—then they see a bright star, pointing the way for them. And it happens that angel's wings guard them. Spirits from distant mysterious worlds come to them. The mysterious Voice speaks to them—everything round them grows bright. They become alive. They revive the whole world.

And so the world has its brightenings and its darkenings, its climbs to the heights and its sinking to the depths, its sense and anti-sense, its ways and its out-of-the-ways. When the heart of the world sees the fountain on the mountain—then the heart beats calmly, restfully, and all the limbs receive their nourishment. When the heart does not see the fountain it becomes weakened, and the body of the world grows faint.

Rabbi Nachman Bratzlaver was not only a great poet, but—and this is the essential point—he was a mystic, and he was also a holy man, a saint, a Zaddik, a man with an unusually purified soul. He looked in everything for God's Light, and everywhere he found it. "In the same way as when we heal one who is blind," he once said, "we must shut him away so that he should not see the light all at once, but we must let the light penetrate slowly, in small quantities, so that the suddenness shouldn't do him harm, so it is with one who has slept for a long time in darkness; when we want to waken him and show him his spiritual countenance we must clothe it in tales and parables so that the sudden brightness shouldn't harm him."

Translated into modern speech it means that art must not be created for art's sake, but for the idea, for the ideal.

The chief point in all the Bratzlaver's teachings was his far-sighted vision of an ideal Messianic order, and his momentary concentration on the effort to bring—in his mystical Kabbalistic language—"the redemption of the way of the Kingdom, which is now in captivity," in other words, the conscience and the emotions of man held captive by wickedness and irresponsibility.

Rabbi Nachman's tales are on one side the story of Creation, and on the other, the story of his own life. But not his outward life, not even his ordinary inner life, but that exalted life of a soul that descended in order to save the world, to lift the sunken, to wage God's great war and point the road to salvation, final and complete.

Here is one of his stories about a cantor, the precentor who leads the worshipers in prayer—a story about the various idols that plunge whole nations down to perdition. It is the story of a country where they worshiped mammon, money. And another country which worshiped cruelty (like Nazi Germany). Another country where they never stopped talking (a parliamentary state). He shows us our world with all its ways, its politics, its false programmes of happiness, and the methods of violence that lead to the opposite of happiness—to destruction. The cantor is preparing the road to Messiah. We see the means he uses to defeat the evil instincts of the nations who war against each other. One of the heroes of the story is the giant. How does the giant save the nations? By providing them with food from the miraculous kitchen, which has the quality that everyone who eats of it casts away evil thoughts, all the wickedness in him. When the nations taste this food which he gives them, they repent and seek the true God.

Rabbi Nachman ends the story with the giant leading the nations to the kitchen with the miraculous food. First he led them so that they smelled the savory food, and they pleaded with him that he should give them this food. Then he led them so that they smelled the evil odor of the idols whom they worshiped. Then the nations cried out against the monstrous stench. And the giant explained to them that the stench came from themselves, from their evil lusts. Afterwards, when he gave them the true food they felt ashamed, and they cast away their idols, and turned to the right road.

"We think," Rabbi Nachman Bratzlaver, once said (and it

may explain the story of the cantor), "we think that when Messiah will come there will be terrible external upheavals. No—everyone will only cast off his burden. It isn't as we think, that when Messiah will come the world will be different than it is now. But what? Everyone will begin to feel ashamed of the folly of his actions."

RABBI NACHMAN BRATZLAVER, the holy man, the saint, the mystic and great poet, felt in everything music, melody. "The Zaddik," he once said, "who is likened to Messiah, comprehends the highest, the supreme melody. With this melody he increases faith. Melody is the source of things and actions. The true melody is the singer's very soul, his longing, his hope, his life, his joy." And the great singer, he "who is likened to the Messiah," is the Bratzlaver himself—who comprehended the "supreme melody."

THE ZADDIKIM CULT AND HASKALAH

IT IS THE FATE of mass movements in time to become demoralized no matter how great the original idealism and spirituality. A sublime human ideal works its way through in the most purified form in the mind of an individual, but when it comes back as an echo from the mass, interpreted and reinterpreted, attracting a mass-following and acquiring a mass-mentality, then faith is transformed into superstition, and sensibility into hysteria.

Hegel spoke of this in the introduction to his PHILOSOPHY OF HISTORY, where he said: "In the history of the world the result of people's actions is often the reverse of what they wanted and intended—what they knew and strove for. People work only for their own interests, and as a result something is achieved that is a natural consequence of what was originally brought out, but which was outside the consciousness of those people and outside their intentions. We must understand and remember," Hegel said further, "that the immediate act may contain something that is outside the limits of the consciousness and the will of the person who brought it out."

That common fate was not spared to Hasidism.

Hasidism, which draws from the pure well of Israel Baal Shem Tov, and had the intention, which it also partly achieved, of rousing enthusiasm among the people and giving them a deeper understanding of life generally, and Jewish life in particular, assumed in the course of time a form which was "Outside the will of the person (the Besht) who brought it about."

After the Besht's death, great men of spirit arose among his own pupils and disciples who saw this degeneration developing and wanted to put a stop to it, but without success. One of them was the great thinker, Reb Shneour Zalman of Liady, known as the Baal Ha-Tanya, after his great work TANYA. Reb Shneour Zalman brought out the pantheistic sense of Hasidism, and developed it into a teaching of monumental power and unity. But his Torah was too deep for the people to grasp, and he could not stop the degeneration of the Hasidic movement.

The deeper sense of the Baal Shem Tov's Torah was never understood by the people. Yet the people took it up with enthusiasm because the Baal Shem Tov gave them their simple faith in God and their feeling for Him. Jews are by nature religious, and in essence inclined to mysticism. The Jewish masses took up the teachings of Hasidism as an exalted expression of the feelings of their own soul. The Hasidic Torah which had proclaimed joy in the recognition of God, which had eased the traditional burden of the commandments that were heavy and gave little joy, was a revelation to the people and brought what was in fact a fundamental upheaval in outlook. It was a release from slavery.

The people had felt oppressed by the power and overlordship of the elite and the scholars, who had no understanding for their daily life and their folk-ways. And they felt that now they were being relieved of that burden, that yoke. All at once the people felt released from these elite, and discovered that they had their own worth. They became aware that a man's worth does not depend on his learning, but on his own soul's purity, and that this determines his nearness to God. The new Torah came as a great revelation to the people; it was something they had not dreamed of before.

The Baal Shem Tov was the great idealistic man of the people who with his great love of Israel regarded the People of Israel—the whole people—as a people of exalted spirit, whom calamity and persecution had driven to revolt. The people's minds still fresh with the bitter disappointments of Shabbatai Zevi, who had promised them salvation and had failed them; their bodies had not yet healed from the savage blows inflicted by the Chmielnicki bands. This period also saw the rise of the Frankist false Messiah, whose movement dragged the Jewish people to despair. Some counterpoise had to be found to save the people from obliteration. And that was what the Baal Shem Tov came to do.

The remedy that the Besht brought was, on the outside, truly in keeping with the folk spirit, but on the inside, it was most profound. The Besht's world conception was purely idealist. In place of the Christian conception, that "In the beginning was the word," the Besht made his fundamental thesis, "In the beginning was the thought, the idea." The Besht's teachings was "The idea is the beginning of everything; and the word is the branching off of the thought." He said, "The idea is the father of the word, and the word is the son." "The thought is called *ain*, because it is boundless, like *ain* (Infinity). But when it is embodied in the word it becomes limited and is called *ani*" (the same letters, differently arranged). "It becomes ego." It is the same substance, the same letters, but entirely different in conception. Only man needs the word. Not God. "The word is man's life's spirit." "Language is the poem of the heart." But up on high, said the Besht, "is the world of pure idea, and there is no speech and there are no words."

When a man is at one with the Shechina and he then thinks of the world above, he is immediately there, for *whatever man thinks of, he is there*, and if he were not in the world above, he would not have thought of it.

Thus the Besht was the first to formulate the teaching, which was later developed in the idealist philosophy, the teaching of complete equality between thought and being, between the ideal and the real— "all that is thought of exists, for what exists is thought of."

This Torah the Besht adapted to the common folk—God does not have to be reached only by learning. He can be reached more easily by devotion, by coming closer to Him with heart and feeling. And that can be done by even the simplest man, one who doesn't understand the prayers he repeats, who can't read the prayers at all. The ignoramus understands it even more easily than the scholar. This Torah fired the imaginations of the masses of the people, and they followed him.

This new revelation was opposed years later by the Haskalah, the Jewish enlightenment movement which, speaking in the name of education, knowledge, civilization and progress, stood put against the "superstition" and "fanaticism" it saw in Hasidism.

But the Haskalah, too, which came out to battle against the ordinary people's yearning for God, would have been powerless to destroy the Hasidic faith, if Hasidism itself had not begun to degenerate.

The first cause of the degeneration was the demand of the Baal Shem Tov's disciples and successors that the ordinary people exercise tremendous spiritual effort, immerse themselves completely in profound thought. But the people could not give forth such spiritual effort; they did not have it to give.

The Besht's successors did indeed promise the people a spiritual lift, but at a cost they could not meet. Hasidism held down that the road to God is prepared, through seerish purity and clearness—by a strenuous effort to go deep into spiritual life that is possible to individuals, but beyond the ability of the entire people.

That led to the rise and development of Zaddikism, It created, or rather there developed, the institution of mediators between man and God—the Zaddikim.

WHAT is a Zaddik?

According to the world-conception of the Kabbala, man is the embodiment of the Divine, the revelation of *absolute Infinity* in limited concrete forms. And in accordance with this idea, the Baal Shem Tov had already, in his time, laid down the character and the effect of the Zaddik.

The Besht conceived the idea of God not as transcendental, but as imminent, not external, outside the world, but internal, within the world itself. God is never out of the world; there are, in all things, Divine souls. But these souls are imprisoned, immured like separate sparks in the hard shell of the body.

Man was given the possibility of redeeming the sparks from their imprisonment. The brook, the stone, the plant, each thing in nature is redeemed by man's eye and ear, is transferred from *not-being* to *being* through man's consciousness, through man's thought. Thus man is a partner in the Act of Creation.

According to Besht's teaching there is between God and man a constant mutual influencing and effect. "God is your shadow," said the Besht. It means that just as the shadow does all that man does, so does God do all that man does. It means that man can approach so near to God that he feels himself a partner in the Act of Creation. Man is also capable through the highest and deepest in him to recognize God Himself, to comprehend the nature of the Supreme Power, which he feels and senses in himself, because he, man himself, is of course a light-giving spark.

The Besht is deeply convinced that man is capable in spiritual exaltation to weave himself into the Divine Eternity, and that there is a mutual effect from man to God.

The Besht often compared man to the ladder in Jacob's dream. The ladder's lower rungs are on the earth, but the top reaches into heaven. The top of the human ladder, the pride and the crown of mankind is the Zaddik. In this the Besht follows the Zohar, which says "the Zaddik is the base of the world." The Zaddik, says the Besht, is like a tree planted in fertile ground. As the tree absorbs all the juices of the earth and produces from them the finest fruits, so the Zaddik collects all the sparks of the world and raises them to God. The Zaddik is a man of higher degree, who raises himself by his yearning for God above the hard shell of the body. He can even annul God's decrees, the strict laws of nature, and turn the way of justice to the way of mercy.

In the conception of Hasidism, a Zaddik is the man who is supremely dedicated to the object of bringing good and redemption, the man whose spiritual powers are purified and without contradiction, and directed to this sole mission. He is conceived as the man whose transcendental responsibility has arisen from a conscious conscience to an existence that can not only affect the fate of man and society potentially, but actually does this. He is the pure man through whom God wishes to become known, to become loved, to become desired and yearned for. Through him man recognizes his own original prototype—the cosmic primordial man, who raises himself to the Sephirot. It is he who averts the great stream of ungood and turns the world back to its pure origin. He is not the product of time, but is above time.

He is the mediator who carries the prayers from below up above, and brings the blessings from the above down below. He spreads over man the streams of holiness that flow from above.

The Zaddik is, as it says in Proverbs, "an everlasting foundation." He is the foundation, because through what he does he unendingly causes that the light of the Shechina should not cease to stream down upon the world.

The Zaddik stands higher than an angel. An angel is fixed. This is how he is, and he can't be different. But a Zaddik keeps on rising. He rises to the very sources of holiness and purity, and with them redeems the world. Continual spiritual renewal is the proper life vocation of the Zaddik.

The Zaddik idea which first engaged the mind of the Baal Shem Tov was later developed by his disciples, especially the great Reb Dov Ber, the Maggid of Meseritz. But both the Besht and Reb Dov Ber stressed that the bond between the Zaddik of his generation and the people must be one purely of ideas. The Zaddik must not direct his prayers towards actual material needs.

But real life is more powerful than abstract ideas; it puts its stamp on them, fills them, with concrete claims and demands.

The profound theosophic conjectures about the cosmic role of the human personality generally and of the Zaddik of the generation in particular, could interest only the select few who were well acquainted with the theoretical Kabbala and with the romantic world of Jewish mysticism. But the masses of the people wanted real help, support; they longed for a guide and a leader who would be close at hand, whom they could understand, and who would sustain them in their need. If the Zaddik can do everything, if he is so loved by God that he can annul the severest decrees, can even change the Act of Creation, then let him show what he can do, let him reveal his miraculous powers, let him in the first place provide his Hasidim with a livelihood and free them from punishment. That is what the masses, with their fully believing hearts desired and waited for, one who could show these wonders, who could, in fact, be their helper and provider. Thus the pressure of the masses created practical Zaddikism.

It was faith in the Zaddik, who lives in both worlds, the upper and the lower, who is the link in the chain between these two worlds, the man through whom the prayers from below are brought on high and the blessings from on high are brought down below—it was this faith that captured all hearts.

So the Zaddik really brought to the believing Hasidim among the people, security in life, and a great faith in God, but at the same time he impoverished their soul of the great value of personally reaching God.

To this must be added the self-deception practiced by some of the Zaddikim. At first only those were crowned as Zaddikim who were worthy of the title. They were disciples, pupils, or pupils of the pupils of the Baal Shem Tov. But a Zaddik must obtain from the community enough material means to enable him to devote himself completely to the needs of the people. This resulted in men of lesser worth calling themselves Zaddikim. And to justify their pretensions to be regarded as Zaddikim, as they could show no great scholarship, they pretended to work miracles. In many places there was fraud and deceit, which repelled the more thinking and educated among the people but attracted the ignorant and simple folk.

That led to the Haskalah, which denied all that had to do with Hasidism, and overlooked the original core, the soul of the movement.

The Haskalah viewed the practical Zaddikim with the eyes of Rabbi Nachman of Bratzlav, the great poet, mystic and man of absolute integrity, one of the giants among the

Zaddikim. He too proclaimed that the Zaddik was so high and exalted that no human act could be right and no soul could find its perfection without the true Zaddik. But his Zaddikism was purely ideal, and he would fly into a rage when one of his Hasidim asked him to pray for his livelihood, or when his Hasidim told stories about his wonders and miracles.

"How have you a heart to calumniate me with such stupidities? I am as one who strides day and night through deserts and wants to turn the desert into a human habitation. For the heart of each one of you is a neglected desert, and there is no corner there for the Shechina, and I look and search all the time to save your souls, so that the Shechina can rest there."

The Bratzlaver saw that there were those who crowned themselves with the name Rabbi but they were not able to educate themselves, let alone educate others. Yet they undertook to guide the world. "In former times," said the Bratzlaver, "the Zaddikim were poor and penniless. Nowadays, they are wealthy. And wealth is of the things that corrupt people. A truly clean and kosher man is very far from wealth. And the wealth the Zaddikim have corrupts them."

THERE WAS a great difference between Haskalah and Hasidism. They were not only two distinct, but two hostile worlds. One one side was the striving towards European education, contempt and hatred for the old-fashioned, backward Jewish ways of life, and immense respect for the outside Christian European culture, for the rationalist world-conception. And on the other, the Hasidic side, was mystical ecstasy, the suppression of materialism, refusal to recognize bounds between fantasy and the real, and complete disdain for the outside world, for scientific knowledge, for alien teachings. While the theoreticians of Hasidism were speaking with enthusiasm of the universal role of the People of

Israel; among the bearers of Haskalah, of enlightenment, assimilation was growing, and it often led to conversion to the Church.

Haskalah and Hasidism, especially the Zaddikim cult, were two extremes between which no compromises seemed possible, and both in their own way did harm to the deeper sense of Judaism.

Later it became clear that Haskalah, which had, according to the Maskilim, in their own flowery language, endeavored to take the Jews out of the "dark" tents of Shem and bring them into the "bright" tents of Japhet, had in reality lost both tents—they had deserted the tent of Shem and they were not allowed into the tent of Japhet, where they were considered alien; they were not received there with friendship, and often they were driven out with hate and scorn.

A form of agreement had to be found between Haskalah and traditional Judaism, above all Hasidism, so that the crown of Judaism should be returned to its original place. A synthesis had to be created which would embrace in one harmonious whole both the thesis Hasidism and the antithesis Haskalah.

It was then that I.L. Peretz appeared, one of the great progressive and national Jewish figures of that disturbed time. He was the great seer who, with his literary genius, revealed the way to agreement between the roots of Judaism and Haskalah—he created the synthesis between Haskalah and Hasidism.

Peretz, who is regarded as the creator of neo-Hasidism, looked with the eyes of the artist into Hasidism in particular, and Jewish folk life in general, revealed their spiritual beauty and sublimity and fitted it into the progressive thought of the Haskalah. Or to put it better—he enriched Haskalah with the soul of Hasidism and the wonderful spirit of Jewish folk life.

THE GOLDEN CHAIN— I.L. PERETZ

*I*N ONE of his folk stories, Peretz relates how once, years and generations ago, a Jew died. He came to the next world, and appeared before the Heavenly Tribunal, which probes the soul's good deeds and its bad. If the good deeds outweigh the bad in the balance, the soul is sent to Paradise. If, on the contrary, the bad outweigh the good, it is consigned to Hell.

"This time a wonderful thing happened, something that had never happened before since the creation of heaven and earth. This soul's good deeds and the bad balanced each other to a hair." The Heavenly Tribunal was in a predicament. What just judgment could it pass on this soul? As its bad deeds did not outweigh the good, the soul could not be sent to Hell. But, as the good deeds did not outweigh the bad it could not go to Paradise. Therefore, the Heavenly Tribunal decreed—Neither Paradise nor Hell, but between Paradise and Hell. Let the soul hover in the middle, between heaven and earth, till God will have compassion on it and will in His Grace call it to Himself.

But the soul was also given an alternative. Let it, condemned to wander, fly low over the earth, to search and discover rare and astonishingly good deeds that men do. When it finds something so exceptional that it is worthy to adorn the crowns of saints, it should bring it as a gift for the saints in Paradise. And when it will have brought three gifts, the saints will intercede for it, succeed in obtaining pardon for it, and admit it to join them in Paradise.

For many years the soul flew about and searched over the earth, and in the end it succeeded in collecting the required three gifts that were astonishingly beautiful and good, three gifts that symbolize Jewish ways, spirit over matter, chastity, self-sacrifice and the glorification of God's Name.

The first gift: A Jew was attacked by robbers. They held a knife to his breast, and threatened: "One move, Jew, and we'll kill you!" And the Jew stood quietly, calmly watching the robbers packing up all he possessed, and it did not trouble him. "God gave, God has taken away," he thought. "Blessed is His Holy Name."

But when the robbers found the little bag of earth from the Holy Land that he kept to be buried with him in his grave, he cried out: "Don't touch!" And as he cried out the robbers struck the knife through his heart. A blood-soaked grain of the earth from the Holy Land was the first gift the soul brought for the saints in Heaven.

The second gift came to the soul from a young Jewish girl. It was, it seems, in the time of the Inquisition, or in one of the many other evil periods in history, when the dominion of Satan completely darkened the little light still left in man. The girl was accused of having stolen out of the ghetto on a Christian holy day and "defiled with her shameless eyes the Christian holy procession, our holy images." For that the Christian court condemned her to be "tied by the hair, by those long devilish plaits, to the tail of a wild horse—Let the horse run, and drag her along like a murderer through the streets that her feet trod contrary to our holy law. Let her blood wash the stones that she has stained with her feet."

The doomed girl was asked if she had any last wish before she died. "Yes," she answered quietly. She would like a few pins.

"She has gone mad with fright," the judges concluded; and they granted her wish. Then she was tied by her long plaits to the wild horse's tail, and—

The people stood tight pressed against the walls of the houses, all raising their hands, some holding whips, some cudgels, some kerchiefs, all ready to speed the wild horse. All hold their breath, all faces are flaming, all eyes flash, and no one notices in the excitement how—

The doomed girl bends down quietly and pins the hem of her dress to her legs, sticking the pins deep, deep into the flesh, so that her body should not be exposed when the horse would drag her through the streets.

A blood-soaked pin from the girl's leg was the second gift brought for the saints in Paradise.

The third gift was of a similar kind.

A little Jew was having to run the gauntlet. A torn shirt on his meager body, and a skull-cap on his half-shaved head. Why this punishment? Who knows? Perhaps a false accusation, a libel. The soldiers smile to themselves and think:

"Why have they brought so many of us here and lined us up? He won't last half the way.

Here he comes now, being pushed into place between the rows of soldiers. He walks upright and straight. He doesn't stumble. He doesn't fall. He takes the blows and bears up under them. It infuriates the soldiers. He keeps going! The whips whistle through the air, and coil round his body like snakes. The blood spurts from his meager body without stop.

A soldier strikes too high, and knocks the Jew's skull-cap off his head. He has taken a few steps before he realizes his loss. *He stops, considers, then turns back. He won't go further bareheaded. He returns to where his skull-cap lies on the ground,*

picks it up, turns round again and continues on his way, quietly,
red with blood, but with the skull-cap on his head. So he goes on,
till he falls.

(My italics everywhere, A.P.)

"Then the soul flew down, picked up the skull-cap that had cost so many needless blows," and brought the third gift to the saints in heaven.

Like unto that soul was I.L. Peretz. He, too, hovered over the Jewish folk spirit, collected its astonishingly beautiful and great spiritual values, the precious stones, the gems of the folk treasury, cleansed them from the grime that clung to them through the years, polished them as one polishes diamonds, revealed their inner brightness and sparkle, and brought them to us, the broad masses of the Jewish people, as gifts.

He drew from the Jewish folk faith, from the well-springs of the Jewish soul the basic motives, the higher will, the whole force of the deeply believing ethical and poetic Jewish personality, and he revealed it all in its most splendid colors. In this story, THE THREE GIFTS, Peretz brought out the holiness of a faith that is dearer and more precious to the believer than his own life. The important thing here is not the objective value. We may easily minimize this: A handful of Holy Land earth. A skull-cap on a man's head. A girl's exposed leg. It isn't the object that matters, but the gift of life for it, the self-sacrifice, the holiness of it.

It is not a good deed that makes a man great but his belief and his readiness to sacrifice himself for it. And this readiness, the self-sacrificing Jewish spirit, among the select few as among the mass of the Jewish people, is what Peretz saw and crowned with his great literary creative gift.

THE THREE YIDDISH CLASSICS

THEY WERE three, great Yiddish classic writers who prepared

the ground, who planted the great fruitful garden of modern Yiddish literature, and whose own creative works reached high literary heights—Mendele, Peretz, Shalom Aleichem. Of these, Mendele is accounted the Grandfather, Peretz the Father and Shalom Aleichem the Grandson.

Grandfather, father, grandson—three generations. Yet there was little difference in time between them. Peretz, born in 1852, was only 17 years younger than Mendele, and not more than seven years older than Shalom Aleichem. There was a much bigger difference between them, however, in their literary work—both in style and, what matters more, in ideas.

Mendele tried primarily to show how Jews stood at that time in the world—the state of Jewish reality within the Jewish Pale of Settlement in Russia. He gave us a taste of that life, what had become our Jewish fate.

Shalom Aleichem had his own way of showing us our ordinary simple Jewish fellow-man as he is, with all his ways and manners, with all his good and bad qualities.

Peretz rounded off, completed Mendele and Shalom Aleichem by lifting the cover, or more properly, the curtain over the Ark, which conceals the soul of our people, its spiritual life. He brought out the wonderful forces that are at work in us, he revealed the endless heavens that rise over our heads, the gleaming stars that speak straight to the heart of man.

Mendele was the Maskil, and his desire was to turn our people to progressive worldliness, to European civilization, to rouse among them a feeling for education and culture, to clear away the darkness and the mould from Jewish life. But that led directly and indirectly to assimilation.

Mendele saw how fanatically backward, how stagnant the Jewish folk masses were, and how terribly poverty-stricken they were.

So he fought with biting satire against the obsolete social foundations of Jewish life. Mendele sharply castigated the antiquated ways and behavior of the Jewish folk masses, but one felt that underneath his harsh words lay concealed endless pain and pity. He reproached and reproved, he flayed with iron rods the leaders of the Jewish community who for their own advantage exploited the Jewish folk masses. But he did it like a stern father who grieves over the evil ways of his son, rebukes and admonishes him, and is even prepared to punish him, yet his love for his child is deep and strong, and it is therefore that his heart grieves for his son's misdeeds. The Prophets, too, castigated the people with words of fire—not out of hate but because of their deep love for them. And when the Prophets' words came true and the people suffered, their hearts were torn with pain and sorrow.

That was how Mendele chastised his people; while he chastised them, his heart grieved because of the woes and sufferings of his poor NAG (the title of his great novel), the prototype of the suffering masses of the Jews; and he behaved with grief and compassion towards FISKE THE LAME (another of Mendele's novels), the prototype of the suffering Jewish individual.

Shalom Aleichem, 24 years younger than Mendele, came at a time when the struggle of the leaders against Haskalah had already subsided, and Haskalah had been incorporated in Jewish life. So Shalom Aleichem rehabilitated the old Jewish world—not by pleading for it, but by revealing the hidden loveliness of its Jewish and its human character. Shalom Aleichem loved his Tevya, his Mottle Peise, his Stempenyu, even his Menachem Mendel, and he makes us laugh at their comic ways, laugh at the situations in which they get caught up—we laugh, but not at them; we don't make fun of them.

But neither Mendele nor Shalom Aleichem went deep into the spirit of the people, into the concealed places of the people's secret soul. This is what Peretz did. He took us back to the source of Jewishness, of Jewish folk life. He lifted himself to the heights of the spirit, and took us there with him.

Mendele was severely critical, and at the same time full of compassion. Shalom Aleichem was idyll masked with light humor and hidden affection. But Mendele's and Shalom Aleichem's people were more or less bond-slaves to their destiny. They did not act; they were acted upon.

Peretz was different. His heroes are loaded with concentrated energy. And he, Peretz himself, does not stand aloof from them. He is one of them. He is *with* them. He gives tongue to their mute lips, he brings song and melody to their dull despair. He reveals the revolt in their simplicity. Where there is clouded vision he removes the illusion from the eye and shows the ascent to the heights. Peretz's heroes are like loaded clouds which send forth lightning and thunder. Peretz is never satisfied with the flat surface, however lovely it may be. He always digs deep down, for it is there that all treasures lie hidden.

For instance, in his story THREE TIMES CALLED, Peretz tells us about a man who—in dream, of course—was called three times. He was called once when he was a boy, far from where he was born, and where his father's house was, Baghdad, the fabulous city of THE ARABIAN NIGHTS. "The lights of the city cut through the darkness. The moon floats over my head, feeling sorry for me, the weak little boy who has got lost far from home, and stands all alone in the open field. But I am not lost. I know where I am, where I am going and what I *must* do. I must ascend to the top of the tower! I must discover the real truth! That is what I have been told to do!"

What is this tower? It is the place where Nimrod is buried, the great hunter Nimrod, who appears in the Bible, and about whom Jews have spun numerous legends. This Nimrod warred against God, and was defeated, and it was decreed that he should sink into the ground. When he felt he was sinking he determined to stand defiantly on his feet

THE GOLDEN CHAIN—I.L. PERETZ • 195

and to remain standing, to go down erect, standing upright. He stretched out his hand and took the high tower and pulled it over his head like a helmet. Let Heaven see how Nimrod dies standing and will not bend or fall at anyone's feet. And the tower which has encased Nimrod's body sinks —day and night, over a thousand years, and still has not sunk into the ground completely.

And the boy in whose name Peretz tells the story begins to climb to the top of the tower. "My heart palpitates, my legs tremble," he says. " I want to ascend the tower! I must! It calls me! I must and I want to!"

The first stage, the first story. A huge room, but empty and dark. A window through which some light falls from outside on the staircase leading higher. Higher up another room, but smaller. Again, a window throwing a thin pencil of light on the stairs leading still higher.

So the boy keeps climbing, and at every stage, at every story, as he climbs higher, he finds nothing more than there had been below—an empty dark room and cold clammy walls. True, the horizon broadens out before him. He can see bigger distances—"a river I had not seen before. A new forest, new trees. Suddenly a shade stands before me—Shemaya Batlan. 'What makes you so conceited?' he asks mockingly. 'You see more. But do you see better? Do you see deeper? And on the top of the tower, near to Heaven and to the stars, will you see better or deeper? Always your gaze will glide *over* things, will glide over the surface, will not penetrate into the thing itself, into its essence, its soul.'"

The Batlan folds his arms on his breast, and says:

"Everything has a soul"—a man, an animal, a plant, a stone, a grain of sand. But not all souls are equally alive and awake. Most souls sleep, enclosed in their hard body, and there falls on them no dew of life. So these souls grow no shoots. But if a soul awakes whatever soul it is, it can become everything —the finest, the best, the highest."

To reach the finest, the best, the highest, becomes Peretz's idea, and his tower-climber goes on climbing higher and higher. "And the higher I ascend, the smaller are the rooms, the smaller the windows, the thinner the light that falls on the stairs leading still higher. But I see each time further and wider.

"The darkness grows thicker. It lies oppressively on my chest. It is hard to breathe. The blood in my veins runs cold with fear. I want light and air from outside. But I am not allowed to stand still. 'Higher!' calls the voice.

"'Who calls me? My feet are swollen. I am short of breath.' And the voice keeps calling—'Higher! Higher!' I climb higher, but in my heart there is a ridiculous thought—'It is you yourself who is calling!'

"I tell myself—what for? What if you do see more forests and fields, more rivers, more mountains, more earth? What if you see more expanse of heaven, more stars? If you go higher you don't get any nearer to them. And the higher you go, the smaller they become, the less recognizable they are.

"I rush to the window. Where is Baghdad, where is my parents' home, my streets, my friends, my Beth Hamedrash? Just dots. If I go higher, the dots, too, will disappear, and I shall be left alone. The higher, the more solitary, the more alone. Where am I hurrying to? Higher!"

So he climbs higher still. To try to reach the top. But his breath fails him. He can't climb any more.

"Down!" the same voice thunders suddenly. "Down!"

"I won't go down!" I answer. And I put my foot down firmly, desperately, against the wall.

"Who doesn't ascend, falls!"

"And down I rolled."

It is the same constant urge to go on and on of which Ecclesiastes speaks. Ecclesiastes had gathered to himself all the pleasures of the world, and he came to the conclusion that it was all vanity, vanity of vanities. Peretz's climber, when he was reaching the top of the tower, also saw that it was vanity. He fell as Nimrod had fallen.

The second call came when he was middle-aged. He had already stopped dreaming. Real life had awakened him from his sleep. "Life, real life, is too hard, too stubbornly insistent to leave room for dreams." It was then it happened, "one evening, a beautiful evening, a wonderful evening." That wonderful evening he again started to dream. "The sun set. It should have been getting dark. But time has ceased. It is neither darker nor lighter. The pendulum of the world-clock has stopped! What will happen if the thread that moves everything has really torn? That what is, remains always, stays in the same form. Nothing moves. Everything is struck motionless—joy, sorrow, pity, pain, anger, prayer— nothing moves or alters. Eternally! Eternal happiness. Eternal grief. Eternal torment. And then suddenly! I hear a voice—'Go!'"

"Reluctantly I move my foot, and everything moves again."

"What is it that moves us?" he asks. "I don't know. You don't know. We shall never know."

The third call came when he was old. This call is clear. The call of death.

Yet this, too is inexplicable—"What is life? Who moves us?" And he cries out to the Creator of life—"Was I only Your instrument, and without knowing it I served Your purposes? Now when You no longer need me, You will destroy me? And I haven't even the right to ask—'For what purpose was I used?'"

This story is characteristic of Peretz. It reveals him both as thinker and as artist. *Will* and *Force*, these are the essentials. And it isn't the will that is directed by the reason. On the contrary, it expresses itself in opposition to reason. It strives to ascend the tower, and is unable to render an account to itself of what drives it there. "Who calls me?" he asks. "My feet are swollen. I am short of breath. And it keeps calling me, each time more sharply, more insistently, louder, ever louder. Not a moment's rest, not a free moment. I want to and I must!"

But what is it he wants? It is clear. The will to lift himself, to get away from the flat surface. The desire to achieve something, to create, to carry something through. And the essential here is not the achievement, but the constant energetic endeavor to reveal new things, to search—perhaps something will be found.

Peretz's endeavor to attain elevation of the soul, the rise of the spirit, is not the peaceful work of the scholar, the man of learning, the rational thinker. It is force, violence, conflict, bitter struggle. It is even war against God, as expressed in the revolt of Nimrod. Nimrod did not win his war. He could not win it. But he did not submit, he did not yield. Nimrod does not yield! He dies standing on his own feet, without fear, without compromise.

Here is another story, not this time of a proud and powerful king, but of a simple tailor. BERL THE TAILOR.

Berl felt he was wronged by God. Let God stop wronging Berl, let Him give Berl his living! But God won't do that. Then, says Berl, I won't serve Him! I have sworn an oath—Finished! No more!

So Berl had stopped doing all that a Jew does in the service of God. He doesn't say his prayers, he has no Sukkah, no ethrog, no lulav. He is on strike against God! But he cries to the Rebbe, to Rabbi Levi Yitzchok of Berditchev, "I am right, Rabbi, I am in the right! I won't budge an inch."

What does Berl want to achieve in this struggle with God? Originally he went on strike over the question of a livelihood for himself. But now he wants more than that. A livelihood is what should have been given him anyway, he says. A livelihood is what everybody should have. The bird in the air, the worm underground. Berl wants much more now.

What does Berl want? "I, Berl, will not submit. I won't return to God's service till God will, this year, to please me, forgive all people's sins."

And Berl the Tailor got his way. He succeeded. Even the war against God can succeed. Man must get what is his right!

What matters to Peretz is concentrated spirituality; that spirituality should overcome all that opposes the will—naturally, if the will strives towards good and not evil. He sets the Right against the Law!

This is the trend in all Peretz's writings. Spirit must conquer over all that stands in its way. One sees it even when Peretz deals with inanimate things, as in his story THE LOG. To Peretz, even the old rotting log lying in the middle of the market place becomes a hero inculcating a lesson. When the log was still a tree in the forest it dreamed of becoming a mast on a ship, on a great ship sailing a great sea.

Ascending, climbing high, will, morality rooted in Jewish tradition—these were the stimuli, the inspirations that stamped their mark on Peretz's creative work.

But climbing high does not mean only the strenuous climbing from story to story of Nimrod's tower. The climbing can also be spiritual, as climbing high through kindness, charity, doing good in secret, as in Peretz's story IF NOT HIGHER.

Instead of going to the synagogue to say the penitential Selichot prayers with the congregation, the Niemirover Rebbe disguised himself as a peasant wood cutter, went to the forest, chopped some wood, and took it to a poor hut where a sick woman lay covered with rags, and offered to sell her the wood cheaply. "How can I buy your wood, when I have no money?"

"Foolish woman," said the Rebbe. "Look, you are poor

and sick. I will trust you with the wood. I have faith that you will pay. And you have such a great and powerful God and you don't trust Him! You haven't enough faith in Him for a few groshen worth of firewood!"

He not only gives her wood, but he gets to work and lights the fire in her stove. And as the Rebbe, so Peretz relates, laid in the wood in the stove, he said, groaning, the first Selicha prayer. And as he lighted the fire and the wood was crackling cheerily, he said, a little more happily, the second Selicha prayer. He said the third Selicha prayer when the fire had burned up and he closed the top of the stove.

The Rebbe's Hasidim didn't think that this was where their Rebbe had gone. They had no doubt about where he was. Where was the Rebbe? Where could the Rebbe be? In Heaven! Interceding with the Heavenly Powers, explaining to them the plight of the poor suffering Jews, winning mercy and forgiveness for them.

That wasn't how Peretz himself saw it. That wasn't how the Litvak, through whom Peretz expresses himself, saw it. The Litvak was the non-believer among the Hasidim, the rationalist, the skeptic, the heretic with whom it is best to have no dealings, because he can lead a man away from the straight path. So the Litvak shadowed the Rebbe to see where he really went when he disappeared. He didn't believe for a moment as the Hasidim did that the Rebbe went to Heaven. "You know the Litvaks," says Peretz through the mouth of the Hasidim. "They have little respect for moralistic works, but they stuff themselves full of Talmud and Posekim."

Peretz penetrates into the feelings of the Hasidim. Like them he searches for the spirit. Where does the spirit lead? Where does it lead the scholarly Litvak elite who go the road to Haskalah and disbelief? Doesn't their road lead them to disappointment? Like the climber on Nimrod's tower. You climb desperately, called by an inner urge that will not let you rest, and when you reach the top you see a wonderful panorama stretching far and wide, but it's all flat surface. And the soul finds nothing in flat surfaces. The important thing is depth. Depth alone gives sense and meaning to life. It sounds like a contradiction, but it is true—depth does not mean sinking down. On the contrary, it means rising up, elevation of the soul.

Peretz never stopped searching for this elevation of the soul. Where could it be found?

He found it in the spirit of Hasidism. Not in their superstitions, and in their ways and customs, not in their dogmas, but in the depths of their souls, in their mystical conception of the world, and their own adjustment to it—in the deepened faith of Hasidism, and the Kabalah, which is truly the prophetic essence of the soul, the deepest expression of poetry of a degree to which no secular poetry can ever attain.

And of the skeptical Litvak, rationalist, practical, Maskilim Peretz has this to say in his story, IF NOT HIGHER. When the talk is of spiritual elevation, of the rising of the soul, of reaching into heaven, the Litvak has "a clear and definite passage in the Gemara, and he stabs your eyes out with it—Even Moses, he shows you, could not rise into Heaven while he lived, but he had to stay ten handbreadths below it. Now, go and argue with a Litvak!"

The Litvak didn't believe that at the time of Selichot, the Niemirover Rebbe really rose to Heaven. So he shadowed the Rebbe, and he saw what the Rebbe really did—how he disappeared disguised, to do good in secret; how he behaved to the poor sick woman. And when the Litvak saw this, Peretz relates, he stayed on as a Hasid of the Niemirover Rebbe. And when a Hasid once said that at the time of Selichot, the Rebbe rose early in the morning and went up to Heaven, the Litvak no longer laughed, but added quietly: "If Not Higher!"

NOW WHEN the Niemirover Rebbe rose "If Not Higher", Peretz, too, rose with him to the heights. Yet when Bontche Schweig came and shamed him, Peretz felt the shame in such a way that from "If Not Higher" he sank to "If Not Lower".

Who was Bontche Schweig?

As Peretz tells us, Bontche lived quietly and died quietly—he passed like a shadow through our world.

Not so in the other world. There angels welcomed him. Father Abraham came to meet him at the gate of Heaven. They prepared the finest place in Paradise for him, and they brought a gold crown for him, set with precious stones.

And when Bontche stood before the Heavenly Tribunal, the Good Angel related all his cirtues and his good deeds. Bontche had suffered all his life, and had "never complained of anyone, neither God nor man. His eyes had never flamed with a spark of hate." His stepmother had made his life miserable. His drunken father had turned him out of the house on a frosty night. He hadn't said a word.

One day he risked his life to save another man, and that man repaid him with an injury. He kept silent. Bontche always kept silent, even when the man he had saved knocked him down as he rode by in his carriage and drove over him. He kept silent even in the hospital, "where one may cry out." He kept silent in life, and he kept silent in death. No word against God, no word against men.

And when the Heavenly Tribunal had heard all this about Bontche, the Chief of the Tribunal spoke to him:

"You suffered everything, and you kept silent. You didn't know that you could cry out and that at your cry the walls of Jericho would shake and fall. You didn't know of your dormant power.

The Heavenly Tribunal offered Bontche a reward—"Take what you wish! Everything is yours!"

And what did Bontche choose for his reward? "Then if I

may, I would like, every morning, a hot roll with fresh butter."

Peretz shames us all with Bontche's answer. For we are
all, every man of us, Bontche. We all make peace with our
sufferings. We hope that as suffering purifies the soul, we
shall be exalted by it. Yet what is the reward that we expect
through this exaltation? When we sum it all up, is even the
supreme exaltation more than a roll and butter? Even a
Kingdom is no more than a roll and butter, with which fate
tries to console man for the great humiliation done to him,
by putting into him the spark of the Divine, wisdom, feeling, understanding, yet never releasing him from the despair of knowing that the inevitable end is vanity of vanities.
And this demand to God, to Nature, to Fate, combined with
the awareness of the spark of the Divine in man, this spirituality expresses itself in most of Peretz's stories. He takes us
into a fantastic world which is all spirit, spirit that pushes
everything material aside, and prevails, even when it loses
the struggle on the physical plane. It is that extraordinary
world where the heart rules over the mind, a world that
treads out the path for Messiah. But it is not an invented
world. It is reality, a world where the essence of Judaism has
its home, and to which—robed in modern dress—the present new generation, too, could adjust itself.

PERETZ STARTED writing at the time of the Haskalah movement, by which he was very much influenced, especially in
the early years of his literary work. Every time he ap-
proached Jewish life as a realist, he could not free himself
from the Haskalah tendencies of his time. But even when he
began to dream of a Jewish life, in the past or in the future,
he was dominated by aesthetic and mystic-religious emotions.

He could not completely reject Haskalah. But neither
could he accept its disbelief. It was—as always—a revolu-

204 • MYSTIC TRENDS IN JUDAISM

tionary period, when sons were trying to topple the Torah of their fathers. The old values were being repudiated, and new values were being sought. Nietzsche had proclaimed the death of God, and the youth of the Haskalah were intoxicated with enthusiasm over the idea of a release from the yoke of religious dogma. But without God, without a Help and a Shield, without Someone to whom to turn for protection in all the torments of life—how can man endure life? If man is all weekday, and sanctity is abolished, where and what is the sense of life? How can man fit into a godless world?

Peretz lived and worked in the early part of the revolutionary insubordination period, when the Haskalah was captured by the Marxist philosophy of a dialectic materialism. Marxism may be held to be a contribution towards abolishing injustice in the world, between man and man, between man and society. But what can abolish the deeper and more painful injustice done to man in the very essence of his existence?

Progressive human free thought has speculated much and profoundly about this problem—in philosophy and also in science. No one has produced a satisfactory answer—neither Spinoza, nor Kant, nor Schopenhauer, nor Nietzsche—no one!

It was in this connection that Peretz produced his Hasidic tales, and among them JOCHANAN MELAMED'S STORIES, in which, speaking as Jochanan Melamed, he proclaims that in this world, "There is no disbelief, God forbid! It is all imagination! The whole world is all faith! Could it be otherwise?

"The world is great beyond measure. Infinite, indeed! And our mind is so small, so tiny, that we look like a man going about in a dark desolate desert with a farthing dip in his hand, that barely lights up what is immediately round him. I stand by what I said—without faith it is impossible! Reason alone is not enough!"

Peretz puts these words into the mouth of Jochanan Melamed, but you feel this is his own belief deep down in his heart, because it is here that he criticizes the "empty writers, who invent stories of murderers and robbers, to frighten people, to make their blood seethe. It is these same writers who look for melodrama and sensation, who invented disbelief—also a subject to frighten the people."

And again in the name of Jochanan Melamed, Peretz adds: "The truth is that without faith life is without reason! In plain words it means—a man who doesn't believe, wants nothing, desires nothing. Such a man is no more than a lump of clay, a Golem!"

THERE ARE, in literature, different schools and trends, with different forms of expression, of style and also of subject matter—realist, romantic, expressionist, modernist, symbolist, and so on. To which did Peretz belong?

He did not belong specifically to any one of them. He went his own individual way. He did not fit his theme to a particular style. He took whatever style would best fit his theme—realist, romantic, symbolist. He often adopted the manner of the Kabbala, and in his folk-tales he has much in the way in which Rabbi Nachman of Bratzlav wrote. Instead of adhering to one special form, Peretz mixed all kinds of forms, and refused to be bound by one single method of literary expression.

This was also Peretz's attitude to Jewish life—realist on one side and romantic on the other, with an added dose of symbolism and mysticism, through which he revealed types, hidden content and concealed beauty under the cover of simplicity and ordinary everyday life.

Peretz was a complex spiritual and literary figure, who set his special mark on the course of Jewish thought generally and Yiddish literature in particular. He was thinker, artist, Jew, poet, dramatist, short story writer—romantic, mystic,

Maskil rationalist, the creator of neo-Hasidism, folklorist, Yiddishist and Hebraist—all the contradictions and contraries were interwoven and tangled in him, but he managed to disentangle them wonderfully, and he created out of them a harmonious whole.

This was his extraordinary genius—as artist, as man, and especially as Jew.

At the very beginning, from his first short stories and poems, Peretz was an original in the way he drew out his scenes and characters with a few swift strokes, in a story of four or five pages or less, and his figures emerged clear and bold, and developed a situation, a drama or a comedy.

Peretz was the great artist who made his reader complete the picture he had painted, with his own imagination. That was because he was so concentrated, so terse and tense; a few short polished sentences, with more hinted at than said. It made the reader's imagination fill in what had been suggested, much more effectively than if he had said it all.

Peretz was never content with the ordinary stuff of everyday life. He always looked for the Sabbath spirit—something lofty, exalted, sanctified. What mattered to him in man was his soul—and in the soul the additional soul which God bestows on man for the Sabbath day. Art served Peretz as a means of painting man not as he is, with his various problems and qualities, but he strove to elevate man, to put wings on him.

As with man, so with ideas. For example, what mattered to Peretz was not the Hasidism as such, but the humanism in which it is rooted, its poetic imagination, its aspiring soul, its deeply planted love, its love of the people.

So, too, with his folk tales. He drew from the Jewish folk tales the loftiness of the Jewish soul, the winged imagination, the spiritual heroism interwoven in it. He found in the Jewish past, in its Jewish folklore, in its legends, in its myths, in all of it the rich material which he did not find in the present.

Peretz tried most of all to penetrate into the world of unreality, the world that can be comprehended through the spirit and not through the five senses. He was the artist who came bearing high ethical ideas.

Peretz was always seeking the wonder-world. When he didn't find it in reality, he looked for it in dream. Many things in Peretz happen in dreams. Dreams or fantasies were the road he trod to his wonderlands of Hasidism and of folk tales, where real soil underfoot was not needed, and where happenings hovered somewhere between the real and the vision. They release the soul from its bond to the body, and unite it with its twin-sister, the Sabbath soul.

But Peretz did not always soar in the heights of imagination. He also saw the reality. Yet in the reality, too, his gaze was so penetrating that he did not just reflect what there was on the surface, but he burrowed deep down into the depths, and drew out of man the most hidden parts of the superman dormant in him. "There are no two equal souls," Peretz says in one of his stories. "There are coarse, common souls, and there are great, very great souls. Some came out from under God's Throne of Glory."

In other words, Peretz had no liking for mediocre souls, that were neither one thing nor the other, neither good nor bad, which—as he indicates in his story THE THREE GIFTS—are not good enough for heaven and not bad enough for hell. He detested, he said,

"Little people, meaningless
If they curse or if they bless,
If they praise or if they shout,
Or if they spit their flame about.
All their praying, all their tears,
All their anger, all their fears,
It is just

Empty dust."

So detesting, as he did, the "little people", the "empty dust", and finding no one in his real environment with the additional Sabbath soul he sought, he turned to the Jewish myths, to the folk tales, to Hasidism and to the Kabbalists, who though their feet trod the ground, soared in spirit in the upper worlds. Peretz preferred to live with the people of the world of dreams and fantasy rather than with those of the world of falsehood. "Let it be the world of dreams, so long as it is good," says a character in one of Peretz's plays, the one-acter THE WORLD TO COME.

Peretz's profound spiritual gaze always revealed people, not in their low material state, but in the height of their exaltation. And there are moments of exaltation—be sure of it—in every human being, even in one who has sunk to the lowest depth. These moments of exaltation are not visible to everyone. Only the artist, with his deep sight and insight, can reveal them. Only one who himself has the blessed Sabbath soul can perceive it deeply hidden in another.

Peretz was the deep-seeing artist, the blessed visionary who revealed the lofty spirit in the utmost simplicity. He was, in this sense, the most understanding prophet of Hasidism, which revealed in the lowest sparks of Divinity, and saved souls from sinking, cleansed and purified them and raised them to the heights. That is why Peretz says in his story THREE TIMES CALLED—"Whatever a soul may be, it can become everything, the finest, the best, the highest." In another story, THE EIGHTH DEPARTMENT OF HELL, he says: The greatest punishment for a man is "when the birds don't fly... dead birds."

Birds that fly is what Peretz looked for everywhere, and what he found—not "dead birds".

THE ARTIST of old as well as of today—knew before Freud and more deeply than Freud how to uncover man's hidden desires and passions, and give them artistic expression. However much a man may try to stifle his lusts and his weaknesses in the face of the world, and even of his own consciousness, they must set a stamp on his way of life. Peretz saw this and felt it. He penetrated to the soul of man and felt it struggling to break out of the limits of its bodily confines, to become free and to soar high into the boundless spaces of the light of the Shechina. This Sabbath soul of man was depicted by Peretz in gay colors. He was able to transmit with exceptional artistic power—with few words and short lines—the most complex thoughts and feelings for which other writers would take pages.

There is, in Peretz's writings, a mingling of poetry and satire, humor and logic. The short polished aphorism is joined with allegory, with the short story, with fable. His journalism was often transformed into poetry, and his rhymed poems often declined to journalism. But who determined—and where—the frontiers between poetry and prose, when they are both trying to break through to the heights?

Peretz is chiefly recognized as the poet of Hasidism—in which he revealed the spiritual rise of the Jewish soul. In short pictures, scenes, monologues and dialogues he brought out the wonderful spirit, the soul of the Jewish folk, of the man in the street who—paradoxically—is shrewd and sharp in simplicity and lofty on the surface. The Hasidic man of the folk may have little learning, but he has a deep, sensitive and warm heart, capable of devotion and self-sacrifice, qualities that atone for his lack of sharp wits and shrewd sense, which is dry inside and is limited in the expression of real life.

Peretz's people of the folk, Hasidim and ordinary Jewish folk generally, are the "dumb souls," about whom the important thing, as Peretz shows them to us, is that "they have a heart. For from the true Zaddik's heart (and not only the

Zaddik's but also the ordinary man's) there streams out the great heart-full compassion for the world. So, therefore, let not the unlearned say 'I am a stick of dry wood. No buds can sprout from me, neither the fulfillment of commandments nor the doing of good deeds.'"

"For after all," Peretz goes on, "God looks into the heart, and all Israel has a share in the world to come—both the well-learned and the unlearned, who know only the 'Hear O Israel', and the gates of prayer are never closed to dumb souls, who cannot understand even the meaning of the words of the prayer, and cannot say what is in their heart to God." And it is just these "dumb souls" who can and who do in their simpleness reach very high, and good deeds are for them no sacrifice, but a plain everyday natural act.

According to Peretz it is nothing surprising, but clear and obvious that an ordinary simple water-carrier attains a higher level of spirituality than the great rabbi, the Gaon (A CHAPTER OF THE PSALMS). A common street porter, without a penny to his name, and ignorant—incapable of reading a chapter of the Psalms properly—suddenly becomes rich (THE SEVEN GOOD YEARS), decides that he must gain no personal benefit, make no personal use of the wealth that has "fallen down from heaven," and gives it all for the poor and for paying teachers to educate poor children.

Peretz's "dumb souls" get their proper reward. His Abrahamel in SHEMA YISROEL, the fool of the town, everyone's butt, who is taken into the orchestra because he plays the bass-viol so excruciatingly badly that having him play solo makes the audience hold their sides laughing, this same Abrahamel is chosen to play the bass-viol above, with the Heavenly Choir.

Peretz was the great master who could sense the most delicate vibrations in the heart of the people, and draw therefrom the great treasures of spirituality hidden under the cover of simplicity. With the short, half-unsaid words of the common man, Peretz brought out the wealth of ethical beauty that lies hidden in his soul. In both his FOLK TALES and in his HASIDIC STORIES, Peretz reveals the light of faith that burns in the heart of the "folk", the belief in the Divine Mercy, the conviction that God looks into man's heart and not into his mind, to probe the extent of his learning and erudition, which can become sophistry, and can ultimately lead to nihilism. Neither logic, nor the reason and the wisdom of man, nor the limited achievements of science can comprehend the world and the universe, with all that is concealed in it; only the simple and profound sense of interrelation between the human and the Divine can resolve the riddle of life, the great mystery of existence, the sense of being as against the sense (or maybe the nonsense) of not-being. And it is not language, not words that give expression to it, but the heart.

And heart—that is a hard matter, to know how much of it is true and how much is corrupt. But corruption applies least of all to the heart of the folk, the ordinary people of the folk. There the heart is more immediately close to the original source of holiness from which life itself springs, and to the spark of God that is interwoven in the very basis of the essence of man. With heart the man of the folk comprehends the world. He comprehends it directly, because between him and Divinity there are no barriers of sophistry, no dividing walls. The worldly and the Godly are one—with no difference between them. God is All, and All is good. There is evil only where God is not, as it is dark only where light does not penetrate. As darkness is bound to retreat before light, so the unclean must retreat before holiness, wickedness before good, and all that is *not* before what *is*, the supreme glory, the essential of all essentials, the supreme positive—God Himself!

If the man of the folk does not comprehend it with language, because there is no language at all for this, not in even the most accomplished of language, he comprehends it with what he does have—directly for the most part—with heart. With this great gift from God, the heart, the man of the folk comprehends the world, which he does not separate from God, and he develops his faith in the Unity of the Creator. A simple thought, uncomplicated by sophistry logical or metaphysical philosophy. And as soon as man comprehends the relationship between his own self and God, he comprehends it as a near and intimate relationship, and he comprehends it out of love, not out of fear. And with his love of God the man of the folk reaches the highest height— as high as one of the 36 hidden saints. Peretz gives us many such examples in his stories—THREE MARRIAGES, SELF SACRIFICE, THE KING AND HIS DAUGHTER, and others.

Not ordinary, not profane, but completely spiritual, uplifted and Festival-like, was Peretz's vision of the man of the folk—an attitude with a living stimulus that is based on the belief that everything lives with the spirit of God.

As for Peretz's Hasidism, he was not interested in the practical Zaddikism—which had already become degenerated in his time—but in the deep inner spirituality of the faith of the Hasidic man of the folk. All the figures in Peretz's Hasidic tales seek and find the sense and purpose of their life in their enthusiasm and in their faith that "God is life, God is joy." (CAIN AND ABEL).

The people of the folk in Peretz, with their deep faith and their way of interweaving themselves with God, are on a much higher level than even the great scholarly rabbi, the Gaon. In the next world Peretz gives the Gaon no more than "the vestibule to Paradise," while "the common folk, who hardly know their Hebrew, jump ahead straight into Paradise," because "the main thing is devotion and faith—faith in His Dear Name."

"Faith in His Dear Name" is what the Hasid lives by. It fills all the days of his life, every moment, every hour of his day.

As strong as the Hasid's faith in God, so strong also is his love for his people—not the aristocrats, the elite, the learned and the wealthy section of the people, but the plain, simple ordinary folk, those "who hardly know their Hebrew," but who possess the great treasure of "devotion and faith."

This "love of the people" found its most powerful expression in one of Peretz's finest and profoundest Hasidic stories, BETWEEN TWO MOUNTAINS.

THE "TWO MOUNTAINS" are the Rabbi of Brisk, Mithnagdic, aristocratic, scholarly Rabbinism on one side, and the Biala Rebbe, Hasidism, on the other. They are two giants, on the lines, let us say, of Rabbi Elijah the Gaon of Vilna and of Rebbe Levi Yitzchok of Berditchev. Through their characteristically differing personalities we get the expression of two unique world conceptions.

It is a meeting of two wonderful worlds—one remote, isolated, cut off from all echo of the sound and bustle of the folk masses, a world that is indeed all Torah. But this Torah, as Peretz sees it, is "all law, without pity, without a spark of grace, and therefore it is without joy, without the ability to breathe freely, all iron and brass, iron regulations, brass statues, lofty rarified Torah for scholars, for the elect few, but offering nothing to the mass of Israel, the wood-cutter, the butcher, the artisan, the ordinary Jew."

The other world, the Hasidic, is the world where "the Shechina rests on all Israel, " where "joy radiates from the Torah upon all, on Israel." In this world people join in unity with nature in one great glad ecstasy, "trembling with joy as they dance together at the Rejoicing for the Torah."

Peretz tells us that through the meadows wandered groups and groups of Hasidim, under a heaven "where little white clouds floated about, actually trembling with joy," and the Hasidim sang a song, and with them "everything sang, heaven sang, the spirits sang, and the earth below sang, and the soul of the world sang—everything sang."

To the Rabbi of Brisk the mass of the people were an impediment, a hindrance to the study of Torah—to be avoided. To the Biala Rebbe the masses, the multitude were like a song, like the melodious hymn the angels sing to God, like the rustle of sanctity, like the glorious expression of the primitive raw-stuff of the Act of Creation, that promises enormously for the future, fortifies the feelings of faith, and lifts the soul to ecstasy.

Peretz tells us that the Biala Rebbe had been a pupil of the Rabbi of Brisk, had studied under him for a number of years, and had then left him—finding it impossible to stay longer. Why? Why couldn't he stay? "We studied Torah," he explained, "but this Torah was dry. We studied, for instance, a law about the behavior of women, or the use of meat and milk, or a dispute over property or money. All very well! Then Reuben and Simon arrived with a lawsuit, or a servant put in a claim, or a woman wanted guidance on a point of female ritual, and at once our studies came alive, and dominated our world. But without them," said the Biala Rebbe, "the Torah, that is to say the body of the Torah, its surface, is dry. That was not," he felt, "the living Torah! Torah must live!"

So the Biala Rebbe had gone away from Brisk, because there wasn't enough life in the Torah there, but too much scholarly pride and the aristocracy of the spirit. The Biala Rebbe had a dream that the Rabbi of Brisk had come to him and said, "I will take you to the lower Paradise." He held him by the hand and led him. They came into a great Palace. There was no door in the Palace and no window, only the door through which they entered. Yet the Palace blazed with light, because the walls, so it seemed to the Rebbe, were of crystal, and emitted a brightness, a brilliance. It was the Temple of the Brisk Rabbi's Torah.

"One doesn't sit here. One goes further and further, " said the Rabbi of Brisk. And he followed him. "One room was larger and brighter than the one before, and the walls shone, here with one color, there with another, here with several colors, and there with all sorts of colors. But they met no people on their way."

"They met no people on their way..." That the Biala Rebbe couldn't bear. The Rabbi of Brisk, the spiritual aristocrat, could be and wanted to be alone in his "Palace". It didn't matter to him whether the people needed or could comprehend his Torah. He lived in his own great high world, lived his own spiritual life. Not so the Biala Rebbe. He, in himself, was nothing. It was only when he was in touch with the soul of the people that he found a purpose for his own soul.

Peretz takes a stand against the Rabbi of Brisk; but he doesn't minimize him. On the contrary, he has great respect for him. He shows him to us as a giant, an intellect, a true spiritual aristocrat. He contrasts him with the Biala Rebbe, who—strange as it seems—rises to mountain height only and precisely because he bathes deliberately in lowness. He is full of tenderness, of lyric poetry. "He was filled with a great longing," Peretz tells us about the Biala Rebbe, "a longing for Jews, for friends, for all Israel. No small matter not to see a Jew anywhere!"

But—and this is all in dream, dream which is the truth intensified—the Rabbi of Brisk, to whom the Torah is the main thing, not the people to whom the Torah was given as a source of life, chides the Biala Rebbe: "Don't long for anyone! This is a Palace, only for me and you. You will one day be the Rabbi of Brisk."

When the Biala Rebbe heard this, Peretz relates, when he heard that the Rabbi of Brisk intended him for exalted lofty scholarship, but alone, isolated from the people, "he became more frightened, and held on to the wall, not to fall. And the wall burned his hand, but not as fire burns, but as ice burns. 'Rabbi!' he cried, 'These walls are ice not crystal, just ice. Take me out of here! I don't want to be alone with you! I want to be with all Israel!'"

This is Hasidism as Peretz reveals it, the true Hasidism, the deep inner meaning of the original primal Hasidism of the Baal Shem Tov, of Rabbi Nachman of Bratzlav, Rabbi Levi Yitzchok of Berditchev, Rabbi Schneour Zalman of Liady, the soul of Hasidism, which is love of the people, tenderness of heart, lyric poetry, ethics and above all, elevation of the soul to a height for which there are no words in language, where it finds expression only in melody and the ecstatic movement of the body—dance. "Everything sang," says Peretz in this same story, Between Two Mountains, "Heaven sang, the spirits sang, and the earth below sang, and the soul for the world sang—everything sang." And in the meadows where the Hasidim strolled, rejoicing on Simchat Torah, little flames "broke out from among the grasses, caught hold of and tugged at the festival garments, and it seemed that they were dancing round each Hasid, with devotion, with love."

Melody, dance, soul, world-soul—this is what Peretz revealed in Hasidism, the Divine that flows into the human, and lifts the human to the Divine.

In presenting Hasidism in idyllic—spiritual loftiness, Peretz brought out the strength of the idealized Zaddik, the wonder of his great personality, intertwined with the life of the common folk, which is an essential of Hasidism, its deep emotion, its innermost light. Peretz also brought out in vivid colors, the deep yearning that the Hasid has for the great man, the spiritual leader, the illusion of the Messiah ideal, which is to maintain the stability and the balance of life before the human world is lifted up from its lowness to the height of the Kingdom of God, to the Messianic order of all-good. Peretz idealized the union of the masses with and their feeling for the Zaddik, the exalted man, the Rebbe. Between the Hasid, the man of the folk, and the Zaddik, the difference is not one of humanity, of human-kind, but of degree. The Zaddik is perfected. Before he is revealed he goes into retreat, wanders withdrawn from the world, suffering exile, making his way through unknown places, humiliated, seeking to come closer to God before he joins himself to the people. He is the man with an intense, ecstatic religious feeling and a longing for the people.

In BETWEEN TWO MOUNTAINS, the Biala Rebbe is full of longing for the people. "Tell me, Rabbi," he says to the Rabbi of Brisk, "what have you for all-Israel? For the woodcutter, for the butcher, the artisan, the ordinary Jew? Especially a sinful man? What have you for those who are not scholars?"

With the eyes of the Biala Rebbe Peretz saw that one who is not learned can also rise to a great height of spiritual life. The chief thing is his level. The chief thing is not the Jew of every-day life, but "the Sabbath-festival other-soul sanctified Jew."

THE OTHER-soulness of Hasidism is brought out by Peretz in a number of his stories. He gives artistic consummation to the deep faith of the Hasidim, their pious simpleness, their every turn and move, even in the sanctity which they put into saying a blessing.

"We," says the Hasid in Peretz's story JOY THROUGH FAITH, "we drink, and they drink." They don't say the blessing. So there is no blessing in their drinking. "But if you say the blessing over your drink, you drink for the sake of the commandment—you fulfill it." "Joy is in the Torah," he goes on, "in the commandments and the doing of good deeds, in the souls of the Zaddikim—in all that draws sustenance from *there*—from the refulgence of the Throne of Glory."

The sustenance from there, that is the true sustenance of Hasidism, the deep sense of Hasidism. Peretz ends his story Joy Through Faith with a tale of a king's son who was sunk in sadness, and no earthly pleasure, no entertainment of this world could dispel it. He laughed only "when a Zaddik passed his garden, felt faint with hunger, and an apple tore itself from a tree, and he said the blessing before he ate it. Only then the sadness departed, and the spell was lifted, and everything was full of joy."

In another story, The Admur of Niemirov, Peretz cries out in the name of a Hasid: "I tell you that the whole world is no more than a song and a dance before the Lord God! We are all singers, singing His praise. Every Jew is a singer, every letter of the Holy Torah is a song, and every soul in every body is a song, for every soul is a letter of the Holy Torah, and all the souls together are the Holy Torah—one song before God, the King of Kings, praise His Name!"

This is the essential mystique of Hasidism, its ethic, its winged soul, the gaze into the depth, that the world seen through the spirit is not any deeper, truer and soul-ravishing than the world seen through the body. This is the melody, the spiritual melody of Hasidism that not all can hear, but which Peretz did hear with his great artist's instinct and his spiritually lofty soul.

Through the medium of Hasidism, Peretz looked deep into the Jewish soul generally. From under the thick skin of superstition he peeled off wisdom, spiritual beauty, clear pure faith. He brought out the innermost Jewish beauty that cannot be seen with the eye. "There is a melody," says Peretz in his story Kabbalists, "that must have words. It is a very low order. There is a higher order—a melody that sings itself, without words—pure melody. Only *that* melody must still have a voice and lips through which the voice comes out. And lips, you know, are carnal; and even the voice—not grossly carnal, but carnal it *is*. Let us say the voice is on the borderline between spirit and matter. Yet the melody that is heard through the voice that hangs upon lips is not pure, not wholly pure, not yet pure spirit. *The true melody sings itself without a voice.* It sings within, in the heart, in the bowels."

And Peretz illuminates this "within, in the heart, in the bowels," the melody that transcends the carnal, and leads to the rise of the spirit, through his Hasidism and through his folk tales. Peretz's Hasidism revived the old Jewish folk instincts to give color to and raise up modern life that is emptied of the romantic. Peretz saw the Hasid with his boisterous and spiritual enthusiasm stand in contrast to the Mithnaged who lives more in their books, in stony greatness instead of in growth and expansion of spirit. He uncovered in Hasidism the reviving wellspring of the heart of the People.

So, too, Peretz evolved his wonderful Jewish folk tales. His folk tales are folklore, reworked the way a diamond polisher brings out the brilliance in the rough stone. Folklore got mixed up in Peretz with Hasidism. The Hasidic way of life is nothing else than Jewish folk life. Hasidic profundity which rises forth from Kabbala is indeed a field both for scholars and for people who have been raised in the simplicity of the folk tradition. Peretz placed no barriers between Hasidism—Hasidism according to the folk conception—and folklore. Peretz's Hasidism is a field of folk life, which is Jewishly unique, with nothing comparable among any other people. The Hasidic belief in miracles and wonders, the fantastic stories told by the Hasidim, the simple faith in the supernatural powers of Rebbe, the Zaddik, the direct relations between matter and spirit, between the lower world and the upper—all has its roots in the creative folk-mind. and being told and retold by word of mouth and, as is usual, always with additions and embellishments, it becomes folklore, painted on the canvas of Hasidism.

Peretz wrote his Hasidic and folk stories with an

avowed purpose: "Art," he said in one of his essays, "which is missing in our literature—art is the soul of a people." At the same time, Peretz, developed the idea that Jewish writers must not go looking in foreign literatures for either form, or—this certainly not—content. "At alien fires, souls get burned," he said. He also said: "If you have no God you seek idols, and these give no Torah... Then you at best describe, write about; to write is *impossible*." (Peretz's italics). "'Writing', 'creating', 'poetry' is religion." And further: "Yiddishkeit is not land, and not language. *Without* Yiddishkeit and not because of Yiddishkeit, it (language) becomes idolatry. The language is only a means to an end. If I haven't *what* to say I mustn't tell the other man—Learn Yiddish. It must begin with the growing Jewish idea. The form will come of itself. We find in Jewish life the folk spirit, what the folk has to say about itself. We find in Jewish life the folk spirit, what the folk has to say about itself. The Jewish writer should take all these riches and rework them through his own spirit. In the Bible, in the Hasidic, in the folkist lies our sole endeavor."

Peretz poured his own soul into his Hasidic and folk tales. It isn't the events of the story that matter in his work, but the inner emotions, the feelings of his characters, and the causes which brought them about. He revealed man's concealed sufferings and joys, the hidden causes of man's fate. And he told us what he saw in ringing, polished sentences. His keen gaze penetrated to the depths of Jewish life and brought out its hidden strength. Peretz saw in Hasidism belief in life, in nature, in everything that elevates and strengthens man's soul. He saw Hasidism arouse joy in Jews, delight, love of the bright world and of its Creator. He saw the love of Hasidism for each Jew, for the scholar and equally for the ignoramus, the wise man as well as the dullard. Hasidism aroused respect for man, the world and man serves God with joy, not sorrow.

The best examples of Peretz's Hasidic stories are IF NOT HIGHER, BETWEEN TWO MOUNTAINS, the REINCARNATION OF A TUNE, THE KABBALISTS and the dramatic poem, THE GOLDEN CHAIN.

THE GOLDEN CHAIN opens on a scene symbolic of life generally, represented through a dismal, cold Sabbath winter's night, when "trees bend and sway, snow-covered branches tremble as if shaken with fear, and the sky grows sad and sadder." It isn't just a winter's night, an ordinary frosty winter's night. It is a night wrapped in fear, promising nothing good, when nature is but the echo of the darkness in which souls are plunged, the soul of the world, even of God Himself:

"Clad in black,
Wrapped in blackness
Is the soul of the world.
The Shechina laments,
And weeps, mourns,
And it writhes,
Drowned in its own blood,
The heart of the world!"

Here enters the Zaddik, Rabbi Shlomo,. a descendant of the Baal Shem Tov, a link in the golden chain.

Peretz pictures Rabbi Shlomo in THE GOLDEN CHAIN as a Zaddik of the same kind as the Biala Rebbe in BETWEEN TWO MOUNTAINS. He is not, however, content only with his own union with all-Israel, with the mass of the common folk, but himself soars in the higher worlds and wants to lift up his Hasidim to those heights. He doesn't want his Hasidim to be

"Little, little people,
Emaciated,
Shrivelled people.

Bowed they come,
Knocking at the Zaddik's door,
Frozen souls,
Little hearts.
To the Perpetual Light they come,
Stretching out their tiny hands—
A spark! A spark!
Begging alms,
A little miracle,
A sign, a hint from the other side.
And each wants it for himself,
For himself,
For his own wife and children,
For his own household. . . "

He wants them too, the Hasidim with their simple faith,
to bear like him the sorrow of the world, "A world that is
sinking in black despair."

He wants them to join him with one mind, to redeem the
world from its sadness, its every-day drabness, from its
"pain and dread." He wants to have no more week-dayness,
but always Sabbath. The world should return to its source,
to the Fount of Light, to God:

"To Him, to Him,
Singing and dancing we'll go
To Him!"

And to back his words, Rabbi Shlomo, the true link of
the Golden Chain, cries out:

"I make no Habdalah!"

He means he will not let the Sabbath end, by refusing to
say the prayers ushering out the Sabbath and welcoming in
the week. He means to hold on to the Sabbath sanctity,
refuse to let it go. Let it be eternally the Kingdom of God!
He will not open the door to the week-days. The world must
be redeemed from pain and dread!

He explains why he refuses to make the Habdalah. He disarranges the order of the world and that "angers Heaven."

"Why doesn't he, Shlomo,
Make Habdalah!"

He doesn't, he says, because he wants to argue it out with Heaven.

Souls have come flying in, he says, to be judged by the Heavenly Court. Have they not become soiled somewhere down on earth? And the souls tremble in face of the coming Judgment. They tremble at the Gates of Hell, which cannot open as long as the Sabbath has not made way for the week to enter.

"And the poor souls,
Soiled and sinful,
Know the Holy Sabbath is ending.
They know and tremble."

Because soon they will be summoned:

"Come back, sinners!
To dread and pain,
To torment and anguish."

What does Rabbi Shlomo want? Does he want to justify sin and prevent the punishment of sinners? No, that is not what he wants. He wants to do away with supposed sin, through which punishment is justified. Like Job in his day, he comes to accuse Providence for having thought up supposed sin to justify itself for its own guilt, for having allowed the holiness of *being* to be done away with and for letting it be profaned by the uncleanness of the week. He, Rabbi Shlomo, will not permit there to be punishment for

"Souls, hostages called back...
Have the little doves
Not soiled themselves below?

Isn't there a wing missing somewhere?
Isn't there a feather plucked out?
They must be examined.
And the Heavenly Court
Stands ready to judge.
And the little souls
Flutter and tremble,
The poor hostages,
Because of the Day of Judgment!"

Rabbi Shlomo comforts them:

"Don't tremble,
Don't flutter.
Shlomo is not making Habdalah. . . "

Rabbi Shlomo is going to wage a battle against the week-day in life, against the abolition of the sacred life. He will not make Habdalah—the Habdalah which sends the Sabbath to its rest and opens the door for the week. Let the Sabbath not go, and the week will not come!

But the crowd of Jews, his own Hasidim, are terrified of this world-upheaval to which their Rebbe wants to lead them, and trembling, they ask him:

"Rebbe, what will be?"

And he answers:

"Let it be Sabbath! Sabbath!
I am by force holding back the Sabbath!"

With his determination to hold back the Sabbath, he means to pave the way for Messiah to come.

"There, he says,
"There sits Messiah,
At the gates of Rome,
And waits.
He can't move.
The wounds do not heal.

He takes off the bandage,
And puts it back,
And he can't go to redeem the world!
And there is no strength to wait.
And he sinks in despair—"

Rabbi Shlomo cries out with determination:

"The world must be redeemed!
Let it be Sabbath!
Sabbath!
No ploughing,
No sowing,
No building, no repairing,
No trading, no travelling."

The Hasidim listen to him, terrified by what he is saying. He will destroy the world!

That doesn't frighten Shlomo. It not only doesn't frighten him; he wants this to happen:

"Let the world perish!
And we,
We Sabbatical,
We festive,
We spiritually exalted Jews
Will walk over its ruins. . . "

But now his ecstasy is broken, shattered. His son, Pinchas, the second link in the chain, has made Habdalah:

"A good week to you, Jews!"

He has made Habdalah. Rebelling against his father. Deliberately or unwittingly is not clear. But he has made Habdalah, and he has brought in the week, and destroyed his father's purpose. His father, Rabbi Shlomo, becomes confused. He collapses.

"He rebelled against the dominion!" cries a Hasid.

"My son, my black son!" cries Rabbi Shlomo.

What happened?

Those whom Rabbi Shlomo called "little people," "shrivelled little people," couldn't live up to his ideal, couldn't go all the way with him. The people look back at the Zaddik, wanting him to go on alone, alone "to Him!" to pray and intercede there for them, and indeed, for small things—"for himself, and for his own wife and children."

The people are terrified of a rabbi who wants "Eternal Sabbath". And Rabbi Shlomo's practical-minded gabbai, Reb Israel, feels the same fear as the people. So, too, does his son, Rabbi Pinchas. He can't see how the ordinary folk can possibly rise sufficiently high to approach the Eternal Sabbath. So against his father's will he makes Habdalah, says farewell to the Queen Sabbath and brings in the week.

Through the figure of Rabbi Shlomo, Peretz looked deep into the soul of Hasidism, into its Messianic ideal, the elevation of the human to cosmic height. Shlomo looks for the Sabbath man, the superman in the Hasidic ideal, in the poetry of Hasidism, his poetry, Through Shlomo, Peretz brought out the essence of the sacred melody of Hasidism, the most living and most wonderful source of Hasidic soul-quiver.

How does Rabbi Shlomo picture the state of the world?

"There is balance on high,
Before the Mercy Seat.
And the balance swings, it swings.
The beam trembles.
A Jew does a good deed.
He commits a sin.
It cannot rest.
Neither guilty nor innocent,
It trembles."

And Rabbi Shlomo wants it to stop trembling, he wants one scale to weigh down the other. He wants to put an end to mediocrity, to the week-day. "Let it be Sabbath! Sabbath!" Let the week-day world perish. Let only the Sabbath, the festival other-soul world, the spiritually exalted world remain!

These Sabbath Jews, these great proud Jews who are prepared to let the world perish as long as Satan is destroyed— they are Peretz's ideal. The ideal of Rabbi Shlomo is to depart from the daily reality, from the reality that is so real and so trivial; the ideal of purification of the soul is to approach close to its origin, to its ancient source, to return to the holiness from which it departed in Galuth.

IN THE Second Act of THE GOLDEN CHAIN, Rabbi Shlomo is no longer there. His son, Pinchas, is now the Rebbe. And as harsh as he was when he made Habdalah against his father's wish, so he is now harsh as the Rebbe. Like the Rabbi of Brisk in BETWEEN TWO MOUNTAINS he is all Law. No mercy. No compassion. His severity reaches such a stage that his own grandchild, Leah, revolts against him, as he revolted against his father's ideal.

Peretz pictures Leah as the representative of the rational, prosaic Haskalah. She is a dissonance in her Hasidic family and environment, a link breaking off from the Golden Chain. She is astray on the road of the Haskalah generation of her day, which wanted to embrace "wide horizons", and suffered in fact from spiritual anemia. She turns away from her grandfather and from the Hasidic ways of her home; she turns away from her grandfather's demand that the world

"Must be all good!
'I purify the world like silver,
With fire!'
Says God.
He sends out the winds
That shake off the sins from it.
His vineyard planted by His Hand
Are we
And the storm sings:

Thorns torn out.
And the wild grass destroyed!"

Leah turns away from his harshness and severity. She refuses to follow him into the world where it "must be all good." She leaves her Hasidic home to marry the doctor, the Maskil. And she justifies herself:

"Outside it shines, it blooms.
Outside it sings and rings so freely.
And here, draped in shadows,
Swathed in cobwebs,
Caught in a web,
Souls struggle and are stifled."

Her brother, Jonathan, who is clearly following in the road of his great-grandfather, Rabbi Shlomo, and who has no heart for the harsh severity of his grandfather, Rabbi Pinchas, warns her by telling her a dream that he has had. He saw doves in his dream. They flew over his head, brushing his cheeks, kissing his lips, and they whispered in his ear, pleading warmly, passionately:

"Believe! Believe! Believe! Believe all good pious
Folk, all in the Golden Chain!"

Jonathan speaks to his sister about her resolve to break out of the Golden Chain and to follow the non-believing Maskil-doctor. He says that the Maskil and his sister had both been in his dream, had arrived among the doves, and

"He, a man of iron,
Eyes of steel,
Glances like sharp knives,
With a knife in his hand.
And he handed his knife, Leah, to you,
And he said, Cut!
And you, my bad sister,
Obeyed. . . "

She obeyed, and the doves who said "Believe!" fell bleeding and died, looking up to Jonathan and murmuring as they died: "Believe! Believe! Believe!"

It was a wound in Jonathan's breast, and it filled him with fear. He saw two deserters and subverters turning their backs on the straight road—his grandfather, Rabbi Pinchas, the man of stern, harsh law, and his only sister, Leah, cutting down belief with the sharp knife of Haskalah.

Jonathan is not only a mystic. Like Rabbi Nachman of Bratzlav, he is also a poet, the visionary of the "Golden Chain." He tells his dream:

"I was in Heaven. Marble all around me. Freshly fallen snow. Clear! White! Everything around me bright. Holy... And such quiet, quiet silver-white little mists, edged with gold and purple. They float onward, turning and twining, high, high... over my head. I look up at them. My eyes full of longing and joy. And in the mists quiver, shimmer, flash and are quenched, hidden stars, flying up and down and round about, golden little twinkling stars..."

There is another stab at Jonathan's heart when his grandfather, Rabbi Pinchas, enters his dream. His father, Jonathan's great-grandfather, Rabbi Shlomo, had applied mercy even to sinners. But Rabbi Pinchas is the complete opposite—he demands that the world must be purified by fire, like silver—and the wild grass destroyed.

Yet the wild grass had grown over his own home. His own grandchild had rebelled against him, and had gone away with the Maskil, the doctor. And as his own father, Rabbi Shlomo, had collapsed when he, his son, Rabbi Pinchas, had rebelled against him, so he, Rabbi Pinchas, now collapses when his grandchild Leah rebelled against him. He cries out:

"Cleansed the world, and neglected my own house.
The werewolf has slunk in quietly behind my back.
And devoured the purest, whitest little kid."

THE THIRD link in the chain is Moshe, Rabbi Pinchas' son, Jonathan's and Leah's father. He is a weakling, physically and spiritually, without his grandfather's quality of mercy and compassion, and without his father's quality of law and justice. He has no quality at all.

So there is no leadership in the Rabbinic Court. Rabbi Pinchas said the world must be all good, but with Moshe it is neither good nor bad, neither innocent nor guilty. And the Hasidim feel lost, like sheep without a shepherd.

Moshe himself feels despondent. He has no faith in himself. "I can't bear it," he says. He complains that he is a poor sick man, who can hardly stand up straight, and they have burdened him with a heavy yoke. He hasn't the strength for it. He rebels against the trust that was placed in him by heritage as far back as the Baal Shem Tov. He asks to be taken to the people. He would prostrate himself before them, confess to them that he is not the leader of that generation, not like his father, Rabbi Pinchas, nor like his grandfather, Rabbi Shlomo. He is not a link in the chain. He has broken off from the chain.

But now he gets a gleam of consolation to dispel his despair.

His daughter, Leah, comes back... penitent. She has come back, she says, to her ancestral stem, "for help." She had gone from darkness to light, but this light was cold. "There," she says, she had left her child in his cradle. He has such eyes, great big eyes, his great-grandfather's eyes. He looks at you with such big dove's eyes, "but he sees nothing. Because what looks out from his eyes still sleeps there, not yet awakened."

She has also lost her husband's love. She had wanted clear light, but she had found that—

"Snow is clear,
Snow is dead,

And snow is cold.
And sends frost through the bones.
Death is clear!
The mystery folded in white shrouds... "

She had exchanged God for nature, and she had found
that nature is "merciless, false." "Law is a chain. Nature a
rope round the neck. The rope chokes you and strangles
you, will not let you breathe."

She has come to her senses, says Leah—and that, it
seems, is what Peretz meant to say about himself. He had
come to his senses, that "The world can't be chance. If there
is a world there must be someone who runs the world.
There must be an eye that sees. In us, in us beats a heart.
The world, too, must have a heart! A compassionate heart!"

And her father, Rabbi Moshe, the weakling, pities his
daughter, but he does not feel strong enough to give her ab-
solution from her sin. He falls before the Ark of the Law:

> "I pray for her,
> For my daughter,
> For Miriam's daughter, Leah!
> And because I am so weak,
> And because I am so fallen,
> And because I am the weakest link
> In the chain, in the golden chain,
> I pray of my ancestors help—
> Help us!"

But "They are silent!" he cries out in despair.
Frightened voices are raised: "The chain is broken!"
But at that moment gabbai, Reb Israel, says: "No!
Jonathan is the rabbi now!"

And the Golden Chain goes on. It stretches over the road
started by the Baal Shem Tov, trodden by the great-grandfather Shlomo, and continued through Jonathan and his sister
Leah, into whose ears the doves have murmured "Believe!

Believe! Believe!" It is a refrain that will never depart from them.

INDEX

9 780824 604738